IMMERSION
Bible Studies

EXODUS,
LEVITICUS,
NUMBERS

Praise for IMMERSION

"IMMERSION BIBLE STUDIES is a powerful tool in helping readers to hear God speak through Scripture and to experience a deeper faith as a result."
    Adam Hamilton, author of *24 Hours That Changed the World*

"This unique Bible study makes Scripture come alive for students. Through the study, students are invited to move beyond the head into the heart of faith."
    Bishop Joseph W. Walker, author of *Love and Intimacy*

"If you're looking for a deeper knowledge and understanding of God's Word, you must dive into IMMERSION BIBLE STUDIES. Whether in a group setting or as an individual, you will experience God and his unconditional love for each of us in a whole new way."
    Pete Wilson, founding and senior pastor of Cross Point Church

"This beautiful series helps readers become fluent in the words and thoughts of God, for purposes of illumination, strength building, and developing a closer walk with the One who loves us so."
    Laurie Beth Jones, author of *Jesus, CEO and The Path*

"I highly commend to you IMMERSION BIBLE STUDIES, which tells us what the Bible teaches and how to apply it personally."
    John Ed Mathison, author of *Treasures of the Transformed Life*

IMMERSION
Bible Studies

EXODUS,
LEVITICUS,
NUMBERS

W. Eugene March

Abingdon Press

Nashville

EXODUS, LEVITICUS, NUMBERS
IMMERSION BIBLE STUDIES
by W. Eugene March

Library of Congress Cataloging-in-Publication Data

March, W. Eugene (Wallace Eugene), 1935-
  Exodus, Leviticus, Numbers / W. Eugene March.
    p. cm. — (Immersion Bible studies)
  ISBN 978-1-4267-1632-4 (curriculum—printed text plus-cover : alk. paper) 1. Bible.
O.T. Exodus—Textbooks. 2. Bible. O.T. Leviticus—Textbooks. 3. Bible. O.T.
Numbers—Textbooks. I. Title.
  BS1245.5.M37 2012
  222'.106—dc23

                        2011046662

Editor: Jack A. Keller, Jr.
Leader Guide Writer: Martha Bettis Gee

12 13 14 15 16 17 18 19 20 21—10 9 8 7 6 5 4 3 2 1

Manufactured in the United States of America

Contents

REVIEW TEAM

IMMERSION BIBLE STUDIES

A fresh new look at the Bible, from beginning to end,
and what it means in your life.

Welcome to IMMERSION!

We've asked some of the leading Bible scholars, teachers, and pastors to help us with a new kind of Bible study. IMMERSION remains true to Scripture but always asks, "Where are you in your life? What do you struggle with? What makes you rejoice?" Then it helps you read the Scriptures to discover their deep, abiding truths. IMMERSION is about God and God's Word, and it is also about you—not just your thoughts, but your feelings and your faith.

In each study you will prayerfully read the Scripture and reflect on it. Then you will engage it in three ways:

Claim Your Story
> Through stories and questions, think about your life, with its struggles and joys.

Enter the Bible Story
> Explore Scripture and consider what God is saying to you.

Live the Story
> Reflect on what you have discovered, and put it into practice in your life.

IMMERSION makes use of an exciting new translation of Scripture, the Common English Bible (CEB). The CEB and IMMERSION BIBLE STUDIES will offer adults:

- the emotional expectation to find the love of God
- the rational expectation to find the knowledge of God
- reliable, genuine, and credible power to transform lives
- clarity of language

Whether you are using the Common English Bible or another translation, IMMERSION BIBLE STUDIES will offer a refreshing plunge into God's Word, your life, and your life with God.

1.
Moses and the Confrontation With Pharaoh

Exodus 1:1–11:10

Claim Your Story

Where there are people there will be conflict. Where there is conflict leaders will arise. Whether in a local parent/teacher organization, in a church council, or amidst a local softball league, conflicts occur. How they are resolved can make all the difference in the future of the group in question and in the relationships of all those involved. There can also be injury and deep resentments. There can be resolution and healing. Indeed, when dealt with appropriately, conflicts can be occasions for great growth.

How do you react to such situations? Do you simply ignore them and go another way? Do you wait for someone else to take charge and resolve the problem? Do you assume that you have no power in the circumstances, no skills to contribute, or nothing really at stake anyway? Would you rather run than fight? Not everyone can be the leader, but everyone can participate in reaching a solution.

Often leaders are "made" by the people they are asked to serve. People recognize that one of their friends or someone in the group has the personality and skills to guide the group in the midst of the difficulty being faced and they ask that person to take the lead. Other times, someone emerges because he or she doesn't like what is going on and decides to try to do something to change the situation. Often the leader doesn't realize that he or she is the leader until after the fact. So as you think about how to deal with the conflicts when they arise, whom might you ask to lead? Do people ever ask you to do something special in the midst of controversy? How strong is your own dismay at the reluctance of people to own up to a bad situation and to do something to correct it? Might you, could you, would you consider taking on a leadership role or becoming an active participant in the efforts to resolve the problem? These are some of the questions that this chapter prompts us all to consider.

Enter the Bible Story

The Bible preserves for us a number of stories about people who were called to lead in times of stress or conflict. The story of the people of Israel begins amidst great conflict in Egypt, where they lived in slavery, awaiting a Moses to lead them out of their misery. The Book of Exodus (in Hebrew tradition, the name of the book is *shemot*, "names," from Exodus 1:1) preserves the account of the events of this deliverance.

Pharaoh's Egypt

Israel's life in Egypt began on a positive note. Jacob (whose other name was Israel, Genesis 32:28), with the help of his son Joseph, who had risen to a position of authority in Pharaoh's court (Genesis 41:37–47:31), brought his family to Egypt to escape the ravages of famine in Canaan. The family prospered until "a new king came to power in Egypt who didn't know Joseph" (Exodus 1:7-8). Then Israel's life in Egypt took a negative turn.

Because the Israelites had increased in number, the new Pharaoh worried that they might join with other enemies of the court in a revolt. What's more, were the Israelites to escape, Egypt would be deprived of a cheap labor force on which they depended (Exodus 1:9-10). The Hebrews, who began their life in Egypt as shepherds caring for their flocks and offering assistance in the care of Egyptian livestock (Genesis 47:1-12), were conscripted to assist in the construction of two large supply centers, Pithom and Ramses, being built for Pharaoh (Exodus 1:11). Driven by his fear of the Israelites, Pharaoh and the Egyptian taskmasters "enslaved the Israelites. They made their lives miserable with hard labor, making mortar and bricks, doing field work, and by forcing them to do all kinds of other cruel work" (Exodus 1:13-14).

About the Scripture

Egypt's Empire

Egypt was a super power through much of the third and second millennia B.C. During the Old Kingdom (2600–2100 B.C.), Egyptians excelled in mathematics and in astronomy. The pyramids were constructed. The events recounted in Exodus probably occurred later during the New Kingdom (1550–1069 B.C.). Egypt's empire extended from Nubia, in the south (almost to modern Ethiopia), to the River Euphrates, in the north (in modern Iraq). What we know now as Turkey was also under Egyptian hegemony. Although no concrete evidence exists to prove the case, Ramses II (1290–1224 B.C.) is considered most likely to have been the Pharaoh reigning at the time of the Exodus events. His capitol was located in the Delta, he used a great number of laborers in a variety of building projects, and Egypt slowly declined after his reign.

Surprising Leaders

In an effort to stem the population growth of the Israelites, Pharaoh decided to institute a program of infanticide. He decreed that every male infant born to a Hebrew woman was to be killed at delivery (Exodus1:16). This massacre of their newborn sons along with the increase in forced labor that was imposed was intended to keep the Hebrews in line.

In this threatening situation, however, surprising leaders emerged who led in a silent but effective protest. They were two midwives, Shiphrah and Puah, persons of little power, directly involved in the births in the Israelite community and accountable to Pharaoh to carry out his directive. It would have been expected and understandable for them to comply. After all, Pharaoh was the leader of the most powerful nation of the time.

Shiphrah and Puah, however, were women with a strong moral conscience. Thus they chose to disregard Pharaoh's order (Exodus 1:17). When the number of Hebrew boys did not decline, the midwives were called in for questioning. They calmly explained that the Hebrew women were strong and completed their birthing before the midwives could reach them to carry out Pharaoh's order (Exodus 1:19). Because of their regard for God, they refused to carry out what they deemed an immoral royal directive. As a result, both the midwives and the Hebrew people flourished (Exodus 1:20-21).

These women did not set out to be leaders; but because of the situation, they assumed an unexpected role in the story. They responded to their circumstance. And in the course of their actions, their names have been remembered; while that of the tyrannical Pharaoh has been lost to history. Leadership can emerge when least expected and from the most unlikely of sources.

Moses: From Pharaoh's Court to Midian

Pharaoh's daughter found the infant Moses in a wicker basket in the reeds along the Nile (Exodus 2:5). Moses was placed there by his Hebrew mother, who sought to preserve him from another decree of Pharaoh that anyone who found a Hebrew baby boy should drown the child by casting him into the Nile (Exodus 1:22). Pharaoh's daughter (whose name we don't know) took pity on the baby, arranged to have a Hebrew wet nurse (unknown to her, the nurse was his birth mother!), and raised the child in Pharaoh's court as her son (Exodus 2:6-9). She named the boy "Moses," which was a play on a Hebrew word meaning "to draw out" (Exodus 2:10).

Despite his place of privilege in the royal house, as Moses grew to adulthood, he became aware of his Hebrew kinfolk and of their ill treatment at the hands of their Egyptian taskmasters. One day, in a moment of righteous indignation, Moses struck down an Egyptian who was beating a Hebrew. Soon, however, realizing that his deed was known and fearing that Pharaoh would kill him, he fled Egypt and went east to Midian (Exodus 2:11-15). There he was welcomed into the home of a Midianite priest named Reuel (Exodus 2:18; also called Jethro, 3:1). Eventually Moses married Zipporah, one of the priest's seven daughters (Exodus 2:21-22). Only later would Moses return to Egypt to lead the Hebrews out of their bondage.

God's Charge to Moses

Some leaders are directly commissioned by God. Moses was such a leader. It happened this way. Moses was in the wilderness caring for the flock of his father-in-law Jethro/Reuel when he observed an amazing phenomenon: a bush brightly burning but not being consumed in the fire (Exodus 3:1-2). When he approached to examine this more closely, God stopped him and commanded him to take off his sandals in recognition that he was standing on holy ground (Exodus 3:3-5). God declared that he was "the God of your father, the God of Abraham, the God of Isaac, and the God of Jacob" (Exodus 3:6, NRSV). God had heard the outcry of the Hebrews in Egypt and had decided to rescue them. God chose Moses to lead the people out of Egypt and take them to "a good and broad land, a land flowing with milk and honey" (Exodus 3:7-9, NRSV). To empower Moses, God did something very special: God revealed his personal name, "I am," to Moses (Exodus 3:14-15).

About the Scripture

God's Special Name

In the Hebrew text, God declares the divine name as "*'ehyeh 'asher 'ehyeh*" (Exodus 3:14). This phrase can be translated "I am who I will be" or "I cause what will be to be." The Septuagint (an early Greek translation of the Old Testament) translated the phrase as "I am who I am" (so do the NRSV and NIV). *YHWH,* a derivative of *'ehyeh,* came to be understood as the divine name but was never pronounced in Jewish worship. Modern scholars speculate that "*Yahweh*" may be the proper vocalization of *YHWH.* The NRSV and some other contemporary English translations, following Jewish tradition, use the term "the Lᴏʀᴅ" whenever *YHWH* appears in the Hebrew text. In his Gospel, John seems to be alluding to Exodus with his use of the term "*I am*" in describing Jesus as the bread of life (John 6:35, 51); the light of the world (John 8:12); the gate (John 10:7, 9); the good shepherd (John 10:11, 14); the resurrection and the life (John 11:25); the way, the truth, and the life (John 14:6); and the true vine (John 15:1, 5).

The substance of God's charge to Moses was that Moses was to return to Egypt and confront Pharaoh with the demand that he allow the Hebrews to leave Egypt in order to worship God at a place of God's choosing (Exodus 3:10, 18; 4:22; 6:10). Moses' immediate reaction was to object. He had not been raised as a Hebrew in the first place and had long been in Midian; thus he doubted that either the Israelites or Pharaoh would pay any attention to him (Exodus 3:11-12). Further, Moses considered himself "slow of speech and slow of tongue" and thus unqualified to serve as God's agent before Pharaoh or the Israelites (Exodus 4:10, NRSV). Knowing the great power of Pharaoh, Moses could not see how he was to prevail in carrying out the divine commission.

To each excuse or objection, God responded with assurance that with divine help (which included God's sending Aaron, Moses' brother, with him), Moses would be able to carry out his assignment (Exodus 3:12; 4:12-16; 4:2-5, 17). We should note that Moses and Aaron were not young rabble rousers when they were directed to carry out God's plan. The text tells us that "Moses was 80 years old and Aaron was 83 when they spoke to Pharaoh" (Exodus 7:7). Age was neither a qualification nor disqualification before God. God didn't ask Moses to volunteer; God instructed Moses to go. Moses was well equipped even though he did not know it. He knew Pharaoh's court, could speak Egyptian as well as Hebrew, and had experienced the pain of the Hebrew people. Sometimes leaders such as Moses are developed over time. At other times, circumstances dictate immediate decision, as with Shiphrah and Puah. Sometimes leaders are prominent people; other times they are ordinary folk. Sometimes they are young; sometimes they are older and experienced. Whatever the case, the leaders God calls forth are always assured of God's help and presence. This is demonstrated repeatedly in the unfolding story of the Bible, true with Moses and continuing with Jesus and his disciples.

God's Outstretched Arm

The confrontation between Moses and Pharaoh is understood as a conflict between God, the Lord, and a tyrant, who considered himself god-like and alone worthy of obeisance on the part of his people. Throughout the conflict, it is clear that Pharaoh makes his own choices, demonstrating repeatedly a kind of stubbornness that the account describes as hard of heart (Exodus 7:3; et al., NRSV and NIV). At the same time, it is clear throughout that the Lord will be the ultimate winner in this confrontation of "gods."

To overcome Pharaoh, God pledged a series of "amazing acts" and assured Moses that God's outstretched arm, a symbol of divine power, would prevail (Exodus 4:21; 6:6). These marvels are described in terms of a series of "signs and wonders" (Exodus 7:3, NRSV and NIV). There will be ten, and the first in chapter seven is illustrative of all but the tenth. Pharaoh ordered Moses to do a wonder. Aaron cast down Moses' rod, which immediately and wondrously became a snake (7:9-10). The contest would seem to be over, with the Lord the winner. But not so! Pharaoh's wise men, sorcerers, and magicians "by using their secret knowledge" were able to duplicate this wonder (Exodus 7:11-12). Aaron's staff-snake proceeded to "swallow up" the other ones; but Pharaoh's mind and heart were already set, and he "wouldn't listen to them" (Exodus 7:12-13).

As already noted, there were ten demonstrations of God's power before Pharaoh finally conceded. The land was overrun with frogs, then gnats, then flies. Boils afflicted both people and their animals. An infestation of locusts followed a disastrous hailstorm. The ninth wonder saw Egypt engulfed in deep darkness, despite the fact that one of the major deities worshiped in Egypt was Re, the sun-god. The tenth, the death of the firstborn of every human and animal, was the most terrifying and will receive additional comment below.

These "signs and wonders" are generally described and remembered as the ten "plagues." Certainly the devastation that Exodus describes is like that known to us in the ravages of famine in parts of Africa or the terror associated with the AIDS epidemic. But the term *plague* is not used in the biblical texts. There is a word sometimes accurately translated as "plague" (which actually means "strike"), as in Exodus 7:17 in the NRSV. To translate that same Hebrew term in Exodus 8:2 as "plague," however, is not accurate. The Nile has been known sometimes to be overtaken with a red algae-like infestation that looks like blood and might cause fish to die, which in turn might bring gnats and flies. But to try to explain the "signs and wonders" by connecting them to such natural phenomena is to ignore the repeated insistence in the text that these are the works of God. They are the "signs and wonders" by which the Lord intends to convince Pharaoh, the Egyptians, and the Israelites as well that the Lord alone is the one Sovereign of the universe and is thus alone worthy of trust and worship. From the point of view of the narrator of Exodus, these are "miraculous signs" performed by Aaron and Moses by the power of God, as they repeatedly ask that Pharaoh let God's people go.

The Tenth "Wonder"

The tenth battle in this contest of Pharaoh "god" against the LORD God is both tragic and marvelous. In light of Pharaoh's refusal to release the Hebrews, God had Moses warn Pharaoh that at midnight, "Every firstborn in the land of Egypt shall die, from the firstborn of Pharaoh who sits on his throne to the firstborn of the female slave who is behind the handmill, and all the firstborn of the livestock" (Exodus 11:5, NRSV). The wailing of the Egyptians would be great, but the Israelites would be untouched (Exodus 11:6-7). Surely, this would be sufficient to convince Pharaoh, yes? But no, such was not the case. Again we read that Pharaoh's heart was hardened and that he would not let the people go (Exodus 11:10). It would only be after the awful event actually took place that Pharaoh would relent and tell Moses to take his people and leave Egypt (Exodus 12:29-31). They did, and they took much wealth with them (Exodus 12:32-36; see also 3:21-22).

There are at least two issues that trouble contemporary readers of this account, both Christian and Jewish. In the first place, what does it mean that God is involved in the hardening of Pharaoh's stubborn resolve? We have here an irresolvable tension between human freedom and the inscrutable will of God. We believe that both are real, but they stand in tension. In the midst of this enigma, the events we call "history" emerge.

The second issue for many is the great loss of life envisioned in this account. How can it be fair that so many "innocents" should be consigned to death by God in order to convince one stubborn ruler? This can make sense only if it is remembered that this action is in response to Pharaoh's decree that all Israel's newborn males were to be killed (Exodus 2:18-22). Pharaoh's crime is punished with the tenth "wonder." To the first hearers of the story, a people who had known enslavement and what it meant to be victimized, the punishment did not sound too harsh.

In the course of these events, Aaron and Moses served as leaders of the people. They stood up before Pharaoh. They took great risk. Their actions sometimes brought greater distress to their own people (Exodus 5:10-23). It was neither easy nor pleasurable to exercise leadership, facing the difficulties that they did. Nonetheless, they served as they were instructed;

and their work provides us with a solid model of what servant leadership looks like. For this we can be thankful.

Live the Story

Where does one begin? Few of us will ever be in a position to lead as Moses did. Few of us will receive a direct word from God telling us to do something on God's behalf. But most of us will have opportunities on a smaller scale to exercise responsible leadership. So how do you get ready to meet such challenges?

First is the whole matter of ethics and morals. Some things are simply wrong and need to be resisted. You can take action as did Shiphrah and Puah. You know your community, your school, your family; and you know whether something is wrong. Will you speak out when someone in the community is wronged? How can you bring attention to the problem and work with others to correct it? Is a teacher in your school browbeating students? Are some students bullying others? Consider ways to make your concern known to those in position to take action. Are there parents or teachers or students whom you can enlist to deal with this situation? Is someone in your family mistreating another family member? Is an elderly person being abused in some way? What resources can you call upon to help rectify the matter? A social worker? Your pastor? Other family members? The worst you can do is nothing.

Second, and at a totally different level, there are always opportunities for service if one looks around. What are your interests? Your skills? If your interest is in music, you might organize and/or lead a singing group or musical ensemble to perform at a local center for senior citizens. Or if you have skill with math, you might join or create a group that will help people prepare their tax returns. There are always programs that can use volunteers from giving one-on-one attention to elementary school children with their reading to participating in Dare to Care or Habitat for Humanity. Service is directly related to leadership. So look for opportunities to lead by service; thereby you will be participating in God's work in our world.

2.

Divine Deliverance and Guidance

Exodus 12:1–18:27

Claim Your Story

Have you ever talked with people who have had radical change in their life situation? August 29, 2005, provided one such occasion, following the disastrous rampage of Hurricane Katrina. In New Orleans, some 1500 people perished during the storm; and many more died from injury and illness caused by the storm. The survivors, many of whom were transported to cities at a great distance from New Orleans, told stories of their dismay and sense of loss. Their stories were heart breaking. Many knew that they could never return to their homes. Everything they had was gone. Whole neighborhoods had been devastated. Their life situations had been utterly altered. They would have to start over, and many did not see how they could do it. Hard times indeed!

How do you deal with such situations? In the face of the loss of loved ones, of material possessions, or of financial stability, what do you do? What can you do to regroup and move ahead with life? Whether great or small, changes in life situation are certain to come and can be challenging.

The Hebrews in Egypt experienced such a radical change. We think of their release from Egyptian tyranny as totally positive. But imagine what you would have done, how you might have felt, if you had been told to pack up and be ready to leave your home in twenty-four hours? What would you tell your children? How would you arrange to stay in touch with your best friends? What would you do with those who are too ill or elderly or otherwise unable to travel? Would you leave a forwarding address? If so, where would your next home be? Then, of course, there is always the "god question."

If God really cares about us, why do such radical interruptions occur? Why does life get so hard sometimes? How can we cope when we really don't know what to expect next? Where are you God? Where?

Yes, these are some of the questions and responses the Hebrews probably had. So be attentive to those questions and to your own concerns about such matters as you read this chapter.

Enter the Bible Story

The biblical chapters we will consider begin with the establishment of the central liturgical celebration in Judaism, Passover, and end with the efforts of Moses to organize and guide the people who had followed him out of Egypt. Hardship, anxiety, frustration, and despair accompanied the joy and marvel of their incredible escape. The Bible reports it all and thereby draws us right into the story.

The First Passover

Chapter twelve interrupts the narrative that has been unfolding in the previous chapters to consider the preparations leading up to the tenth "wonder." The tone changes as liturgical instructions are given for the observance of what is to become an annual commemoration of the events that are to follow. The sacrifice and meal that are described are known as Passover, scheduled for the tenth day of the first month of the year (in Hebrew, *Abib* or *Nisan*). This liturgical year began in the spring (Exodus 12:2-3). The civil calendar begins the first month of the year in the fall (in Hebrew, *Ethanim* or *Tishri*), which is the seventh month in the liturgical calendar. Today's Jews, following the civil calendar, celebrate New Year in the fall and Passover in the spring.

Explicit instructions were given. A unblemished, yearling, male lamb was to be selected on the tenth of the month by each household that could afford to do so. At twilight on the fourteenth day, the lamb was to be slaughtered (Exodus 12:3-6). The whole lamb was to be roasted that night. All of the people gathered were to dress in preparation for a journey so that they could leave hurriedly (see Exodus 12:43-49 for who could participate). They were instructed to eat all of the lamb if possible. If any remained, it was to be destroyed by fire (Exodus 12:8-10). Each Hebrew home was to be marked with the blood of the lamb so that the inhabitants would be protected when the first-born of Egypt were struck down (Exodus 12:12-13). The Israelites were to "observe this ritual...for all time" (Exodus 12:24). When their children would later ask about the rite, the adults were to say, "'It is the passover sacrifice to the LORD, for he passed over the houses of the Israelites in Egypt, when he struck down the Egyptians but spared our houses'" (Exodus 12:26-27, NRSV; see also 13:14-16). A second festival also became associated with Passover, namely the Feast of Unleavened Bread (Exodus 12:18-20; 13:3-10; see also Matthew 26:17; Luke 22:1). This celebration, an agricultural-based festival, was probably connected to Passover after Israel entered the land of Canaan and began to till the land.

Across the Testaments

The Passover in the New Testament

The rite of Passover continues to be observed to this day among Jews around the world as the defining Jewish festival of redemption and freedom. It serves to bind each generation to the succeeding one and continues to aid in the ongoing struggle against decimation. It is also remembered by Christians, not as a liturgical celebration, but because in the New Testament Jesus is described as "the paschal lamb" (John 1:29; 1 Corinthians 5:7). What's more, Jesus' death and resurrection took place at the time of the Passover in Jerusalem, with the Lord's Supper especially connected to the festival (Matthew 26:26-28; 1 Corinthians 11:23-26). And John 19:36, in the description of the body of Jesus being taken down from the cross, makes apparent reference to Exodus 12:46.

The Departure From Egypt

As noted in the previous session, death did sweep through Egypt and Pharaoh did capitulate (Exodus 12:31-32). The Hebrew people, following the night of the Passover, fled the land where they had sojourned for more than four hundred years (Exodus 12:40-41). There are two accounts of what happened, one older, written in poetic form (Exodus 15:1-18), and a second prose rendering later (Exodus 14:1-31). The older poem makes no claim to be "historical"; whereas, the prose account, by its style, has at times suggested to some that it be read as literal history. A careful consideration, however, seems to make clear that metaphor and poetic license are to be found in each.

In the older account of Israel's departure from Egypt, God is pictured as a mighty warrior who overcomes hostile forces (Exodus 15:2-3). A brief victory song attributed to Moses' sister Miriam is recorded in Exodus 15:20 (see also 15:1): "Sing to the LORD, for he has triumphed gloriously; horse and rider he has thrown into the sea" (NRSV). This may be the kernel of tradition around which the longer poem was fashioned. The term translated "Red Sea" is actually "Reed Sea" in Hebrew (Exodus 15:4). At any rate, God "shattered the enemy" with a strong right hand (Exodus 15:6, NRSV and NIV). They were consumed as rubble by a fire (Exodus 15:7). God snorted, and "the surging waters stood firm like a wall; the deep waters congealed in the heart of the sea" (Exodus 15:8, NIV). When the enemy pursued Israel, God blew the sea back on them and "they sank like lead in the towering waters" (Exodus 15:10). They were utterly "swallowed" by the earth (Exodus 15:12). What a powerful, if sometimes contradictory, poetic metaphor!

The later prose account fills in some gaps left by the poetic description of the departure. It is made clear that Pharaoh changed his mind and sent some portion of his military in hot pursuit of the Israelites (Exodus 14:5-9). The Egyptians were fast approaching, with the Israelites unable to go forward because of the "sea" (not at first identified in the Hebrew text as the "Reed Sea"; Exodus 14:2). The people failed in their trust and turned against Moses (Exodus 14:11-12), but he assured them that God would fight for them if they would "just keep still" (Exodus 14:13-14). When at God's instruction Moses stretched out his hand, the sea divided, with the waters forming a wall on either side to allow the Israelites to cross on dry ground (Exodus 14:16, 22; but see 14:21). When the Egyptian military tried to follow, the waters returned and all were drowned (Exodus 14:26-28; but see 14:25). This incredible event was aimed at making one point clear: "The LORD rescued Israel from the Egyptians that day" and the "people were in awe of the LORD, and they believed in the LORD and in his servant Moses" (Exodus 14:30-31). That was the reason for the confrontation with Pharaoh from the outset: to demonstrate who indeed was God. The LORD prevailed, and deliverance was accomplished.

The Crossing of the Sea

There is no way to identify absolutely where the crossing of the "sea" took place. In Hebrew, the body of water is called the "Reed Sea," which is probably a reference to the marshy area somewhere near what is now the Suez Canal. Those who translated the Hebrew text into Greek, in what is known as the Septuagint, thought that the reference was to the "Red Sea," a considerably different body of water. Some have tried to explain the event in naturalistic terms, noting that there is historical evidence of the waters in the marsh being pushed back by strong winds; but that is to diminish the marvel claimed in the tradition. Where ever, how ever, the deliverance at the "Reed Sea" was considered the work of God and was celebrated as such.

How Quickly People Forget

Have you ever noticed how quickly today's problems can push aside yesterday's successes? The people had escaped pursuit by elements of the most powerful army of the day. They had defied Pharaoh and lived to tell about it. But they had rushed out into a harsh wilderness. They didn't know where they were going or what lay ahead. Their old life situation was unalterably, radically changed. In Egypt, the water supply was totally dependent upon the Nile River. Once that was left behind, all that one could count on were various oases scattered about the desert. Without experience in the area, finding water was a difficult and crucial matter.

The Hebrews had been on the road for about three days, when they exhausted the water they had taken with them when they bolted Egypt. The situation was getting desperate. Then they saw in the distance an oasis, and their hopes soared. When they reached the place, however, they found it rightly named, Marah (Hebrew for "bitter"), because the water was not potable (Exodus 15:23). The people began to blame Moses for this unfortunate turn of events, loudly complaining, "What will we drink?" (Exodus 15:24). Moses, in turn, "cried out to the LORD" and was instructed to put a special kind of "tree" or bush into the water. When he did so, the water became sweet and life-giving (Exodus 15:25). As further demonstration of divine guidance, when the people left Marah (a site whose location is presently unknown), they were led to Elim (often identified as Wadi Gharandel, a little more than sixty miles southeast of Suez), where they found more than enough good water and even ample shade (Exodus 15:27).

Discontentment, however, sprang up again as soon as the people left Elim. At a site named Rephedim (as yet unidentified), the people "argued with Moses," saying, "Why did you bring us out of Egypt to kill us, our children, and our livestock with thirst?" (Exodus 17:1-3). Again, God remedied the situation by having Moses take some of the elders on ahead to Horeb. He was told to strike "the rock at Horeb." When he did, water gushed forth "while Israel's elders watched" and the needs of the people were met (Exodus 17:5-6).

A second difficulty was the increasing need for food. As the water supplies had run out, so did the food that the people had brought with them. Before they had gone very far, the people were charging Moses and Aaron with intentionally bringing them out into the desert "to starve this whole assembly to death" (Exodus 16:3). They remembered the food they had had while they were in Egypt, but they apparently had forgotten the physical and spiritual abuse that was slowly but surely killing them. How quickly today difficulties push yesterdays' miseries out of mind!

Moses immediately responded by declaring that God would bring relief on the very next day (Exodus 16:6-7). And indeed, a double miracle occurred when a large number of quail flew into the camp, providing meat (Exodus 16:13), and a mysterious bread-like substance (which the people called "manna," which in Hebrew means "what is it?") covered the ground (Exodus 16:14-15). The manna was described as "like coriander seed, white, and tasted like honey wafers" (Exodus 16:31). Such providential gifts fed the people throughout their many years in the wilderness (Exodus 16:33-35).

A Lesson in Listening

In Hebrew, one word means both "hearing" and "obeying." If one indeed does "hear," then one will "obey" and act in accordance with what one has heard. In English, the term *listen* functions somewhat in the same manner. To "hear" is not the same as to "listen." "Listening" implies understanding and subsequent appropriate behavior. The account regarding the gathering of the manna offers insight.

The text tells us that God wanted to "test" the willingness of the people to follow the instruction Moses was told to give (Exodus 16:4). The people were told that they were to gather enough manna each day for their needs for that day. On the sixth day, they were to gather enough for two days because manna would not be provided on the seventh or Sabbath day (Exodus 16:5-6, 22-26). The instructions were clear, but some people gathered more than they needed. Perhaps they remembered times when food was not available, so they wanted to protect against that possibility. Or maybe they were simply greedy. At any rate, any unneeded manna rotted overnight. On the other hand, some didn't gather enough. (Were they lazy or inept?) The people were being instructed on how to "listen" to God, how to hear and act obediently. They did not actually meet God's expectations yet (see Exodus 16:28). Nonetheless, by divine grace, all of the needs of the people were met (Exodus 16:16-21), giving the prayer that some of us have learned much later—"give us this day our daily bread"—added significance as well.

Guidance From Jethro

In Chapter One, we met Jethro (also known as Reuel). He was a Midianite (Judges 4:11 identifies him as a Kenite) priest and leader who became Moses' father-in-law. As Moses and the people moved across the arid wilderness, Jethro, who had heard of the wondrous things that God had done, came with Moses' wife and children to meet Moses. Moses reported all that had occurred since he left his family to return to Egypt. Jethro rejoiced, expressed his own conviction concerning the greatness of YHWH, the Lord, and offered sacrifices of thanksgiving (Exodus 18:1-12). Although he had not been present when Israel was delivered from Egypt, Jethro raised his praise on the basis of the witness of others, beginning a long line of people who, to this day, celebrate God's redemption "second hand," as it were.

Jethro observed how Moses was becoming exhausted in his efforts to address the concerns of his people. The people thought that Moses alone should settle all of their disputes. Jethro intervened and pointed out the futility of such a process. No one could do all the work alone (Exodus 18:13-18).

It was certainly Moses who was to intercede before God on behalf of the people and to teach them "the way they are supposed to go and the things they are supposed to do" (Exodus 18:19-20). But the day-to-day work, Jethro suggested, should be delegated to others. Moses was to choose "capable persons who respect God" and are "trustworthy and not corrupt." They were, in turn, to determine the seriousness of the problems, with only the most important issues being brought to Moses (Exodus 18:21-22). Moses took Jethro's advice and developed an effective committee system to distribute the workload in order that others could help (Exodus 18:24-26).

It is interesting that in the midst of this long narrative relating the mysterious, miraculous deliverance of Israel from Egypt, with all of the wonders there witnessed, we have a very down-to-earth, pragmatic, human example of problem-solving. The division of labor suggested by Jethro was an obvious solution to a real problem—at least, it was obvious after he pointed it out.

We need to remember, however, that Moses and his people had experienced a radical change in their life situation. They had been allowed to rule themselves in Egypt in only very limited ways. Now they had to build a new social order from scratch, and they had to do so in the midst of a sense of grief and uncertainty concerning the future. Yes, grief. As bad as the drudgery of Egypt was, the Israelites at least had a sense of security. Now they had to try to start over, with no concrete assurances. No easy job!

From a biblical point of view, however, it should not be surprising when humans solve difficult problems. God expects us to do just that. God is not always going to do things for us. God has given us the capacity and the freedom to develop appropriate action. When we are challenged to begin anew, God will be with us; but it remains our responsibility to act. Jethro, along with Moses, provides a striking example.

Live the Story

The story of Israel's deliverance from Egypt and the divine guidance the people received in their trek across the wilderness is inspiring. It is worthy of a joyous celebration. But the narrative does not indicate that, for the most part, celebration was the response. Yes, they sang a victory song at the edge of the Sea of Reeds; but then they immediately cowered before the approaching forces of Pharaoh. They complained and doubted. How can we understand this juxtaposition of attitudes and emotions?

In part, it has to do with what we all experience when our worlds become radically altered. How do you feel in the face of the death of a loved one? Yes, we believe that God cares for us even in death; but our wife, husband, son, daughter, mother, father are gone. What do you do if you lose your home to physical disaster or financial catastrophe? All you have worked for is gone, and you have no magic wand to wave that will restore it. In such situations, most of us flounder a bit—at least for a while—while we try to pick up the pieces to move on.

Perhaps a way to enter this story in Exodus is to talk with someone who has experienced some communal or personal disaster. Are there refugees in your community who could come to talk about how it feels to start over in a new country, where the language is new and the customs are strange? Could you organize or join a work group going to assist in the recovery efforts for survivors of a tornado or a flood or an earthquake or a fire? Can you arrange to visit with someone who has lost his or her job or who has been diagnosed with cancer? These people have had their worlds altered, just as the Israelites had theirs turned upside-down. Try to imagine what it feels like. What are the difficulties? What are the theological questions that spring up and what concrete answers are to be offered? Israel's redemption was marvelous, but it required them to leave behind all that they had. To be reborn is as painful as it is wonderful.

3.

God's Covenant With Israel

Exodus 19:1–31:18

Claim Your Story

How many contracts do you have? A home mortgage? An auto loan? Student loans? How many agreements have you made with others? Is marriage "contractual"? How about child-rearing? How about participation at church? How about civic responsibilities? What happens if you do not fulfill your contractual responsibilities? Can you be sued? Can you be arrested? Will people lose confidence in you as a person? Will your own self-esteem suffer?

Most of us live with myriad legal and informal contracts. In a different time and place, we might well talk about these contracts and agreements as covenants. But by whatever name, agreements are a necessary part of modern life. Imagine being unable to write a check or to pay bills online because you do not have an agreement with a bank to process such payments. What if you could not use a charge or debit card to purchase your gas, pay a restaurant bill, or buy tickets to the theatre or ball game? Covenants or agreements or contracts are important in the lives of most of us.

Do contracts carry obligations? What is all the fine print about? Do you ever read it? Have you ever been surprised by an obligation you unknowingly assumed? Some contracts require more of one party than another, but there are almost always some expectations that contracting parties are to fulfill. Even in the good old days, when an agreement was concluded with only a handshake, did anyone ever think that he or she could simply ignore the implicit obligations signaled by that act? Of course not! An agreement or contract is a promise. How do you want to be known: as a promise keeper or a contract breaker? That is why it is important to consider any agreement closely in order to understand exactly what is expected and be prepared to honor it fully.

Enter the Bible Story

The amazing power and grace of God was fully experienced at the Reed Sea, which marked the culmination of Moses' confrontation of Pharaoh. The people were delivered, but much more was in store for them. On a mountain known variously as Sinai or Horeb, located somewhere (the exact location is debated) to the east of Egypt, another extraordinary event was to occur. This was to become foundational for the relationship of God with Israel, a connection that lasts to the present day.

The Preparations

Three months after the Israelites left Egypt they arrived in the wilderness of Sinai (Exodus 19:1-2). They probably had no idea why they had travelled to this remote place. As the people settled in to their new campsite, Moses ascended the mountain and "went up to God" (Exodus 19:3). There Moses learned from God what to tell the people. He was to remind them that by divine initiative they had been taken out of Egypt as "on eagles' wings" and had come safely to Sinai. They were to become God's "most precious possession out of all the peoples" bound to God in covenant (Exodus 19:5). They were to be "a priestly kingdom and a holy nation" (Exodus 19:6, NRSV). In other words, they were to be both a civil kingdom and religious priests. In response to Moses' declaration of God's intentions, the people responded, "Everything that the LORD has said we will do" (Exodus 19:8).

To prepare the people for their encounter with God, Moses had them wash their clothes (Exodus 19:10, 14). This was a ritual sign of leaving the old behind in expectation of new things to come. But no one was to ascend or even touch the mountain lest they become contaminated. Any person or animal that did so was to be stoned or killed with arrows (Exodus 19:12-13). Further, no male was to have any contact with a female. No reason for this is given, but it does demonstrate a "maleness" of ancient society that seems quite strange to contemporary people (Exodus 19:15). God was going to descend on the mountain "for all the people to see" and they had to be ready (Exodus 19:11). Israel was about to have a mountain-top experience quite different from what we tend to associate with that term.

The Appearance of God

"When morning dawned on the third day, there was thunder, light-ning, and a thick cloud on the mountain, and a very loud blast of a horn. All the people in the camp shook with fear" (Exodus 19:16). In the lan-guage of scholars, this is the beginning of a theophany, or an appearance of God. Was the imagery drawn from viewing an erupting volcano or a violent mountain thunderstorm? Possibly, but there is no way to know for certain. What is clear is that it terrified the people. All were warned once again not to approach the mountain; even the priests had to be especially careful. Only Moses and Aaron were allowed to ascend the holy mountain (Exodus 19:21-24).

No words are sufficient to describe God. God's presence was both fascinating and terrifying. For many modern folk, the term *god* has become so vacuous that this narrative in Exodus is practically unbelievable. Contrary to contemporary considerations about the divine, however, the LORD God cannot be domesticated. We cannot control the divine. God comes when God chooses and God's appearing is overpowering even while it is indescribable. God is God, and God's ways are not human ways.

God's Covenant With Israel

God appeared on Mount Sinai for the purpose of establishing a covenant with Israel (Exodus 19:5). Prior to this, the Israelites had been special to God as the descendants of the family that began with Abraham and Sarah. God had made promises to Abraham, Isaac, and Jacob (Genesis 15:5; 17:7-8; 26:24; 28:13-15). God remembered those promises and acted to deliver Israel from their suffering under Pharaoh. But now a new relationship was to be established: God would covenant with Israel.

About the Scripture

Two Types of Covenant

Two basic types of covenant or contract are found in the Bible. The first, found in Genesis in God's promises to the forebears of Israel, is what is called a promissory covenant. This kind of covenant was usually made by a king or a nobleman who gave land outright, with no stipulations, to a servant, in recognition of special service. The second type was a covenant of obligation, patterned after what are known as suzerainty treaties, developed among the Hittites in the area of modern Turkey during the fourteenth century B.C. and the Assyrians in the area of modern Iraq during the seventh century B.C. These international treaties were covenants between a more powerful king, the suzerain, or overlord, and less-powerful (usually conquered) underlings or vassals. After a recitation of the history of the parties, pledges were exchanged, where the more powerful agreed to protect and ensure peace for the less powerful, who in return pledged to carry out various stipulations, including the paying of and assisting the suzerain in whatever ways were requested.

The covenant, as presented in Exodus, follows the pattern of an international treaty called a suzerainty treaty. The new commitment between the covenanting parties is based on a history of relationship between the participants, and this is articulated for all to remember (Exodus 3–18). There follows a set of stipulations that describe the mutual obligations of the participants (Exodus 20–23). God committed to offer care and protection, and Israel was obligated to live in God's way. Obedience on Israel's part was expected, but this did not "earn" them the covenant with God.

The covenant was freely initiated and enacted by God; Israel had the responsibility and freedom to accept or reject it. God accepted the responsibility to be Israel's God. With a sacrifice and a dashing of blood on the altar and on the people, the covenant was sealed (Exodus 24:5-8). Then a most extraordinary report is told in a most casual manner: seventy elders of Israel, along with Moses, Aaron, Dadab and Abihu (two of Aaron's sons) "saw the God of Israel." Although they "saw" God, no attempt was made to describe God, only that God stood on "something like a pavement of sapphire stone, like the very heaven for clearness" (Exodus 24:10, NRSV; see Ezekiel 1:4-28). Yes, they "beheld God, and they ate and drank"; and God did not lay a hand on any of them (Exodus 24:11,

NRSV). Later, the tradition will insist that no one can see God and live (Exodus 33:20); but that is not what is presented here. With this most unusual report of a meal, the covenant was ratified by God and the people.

Covenant in the Old and New Testaments

The term *testament* is drawn from Latin and was used to refer to the covenants found in the Hebrew Bible. Thus, we have the "Old Testament" based on covenants made by God with Abraham (Genesis 15), David (2 Samuel 7), and the people of Israel at Mount Sinai (Exodus 19–24). But we also have the "New Testament" that came into being as a result of the life, death, and resurrection of Jesus Christ. Reference is made to such a covenant in reference to the Lord's Supper (Mark 14:24; 1 Corinthians 11:25). The followers of Christ were understood as ministers of the new covenant (2 Corinthians 3:6), a covenant Christians believed to have been envisioned by the prophet Jeremiah (Jeremiah 31:31). The new covenant, the new "testament," did not annul the old testament (see Luke 1:72; Acts 3:25; Galatians 3:17); but it did open the door for all the world to enter into a deep, life-securing relationship with God. The Letter to the Hebrews makes the most extensive use of covenant language in the New Testament (see Hebrews 7:22; 8:8-13; 9:15; 12:24).

Covenant Stipulations: The Ten Words

As already noted, suzerain treaties or covenants always had stipulations, the obligations that the covenant partners were to honor. Usually, the instructions were much more detailed with respect to the lesser party, the vassal. That is clearly the case in the covenant of obligation described in Exodus. God promised generally to guide and protect, but much more detailed instructions were given concerning what was expected of the people of Israel.

The first set of stipulations is what Christians usually call the Ten Commandments. In Hebrew, they are termed the *Ten Words*. They are found in two versions, essentially the same but with minor differences, one in Exodus 20:1-17 and the other in Deuteronomy 5:6-21. We are told that Moses entered the dense cloud that covered Sinai (Exodus 20:21; 24:18). When he came forth, he carried two stone tablets on which the Ten Words had been inscribed by the very "finger of God" (Exodus 24:12; 31:18, NRSV; 32:25-16).

These commandments are what scholars call apodictic laws. They are universal, fitting any setting, and absolute, without exceptions. "You shall ..." or "You shall not ..." is the language used for this type of commandment. These commandments stand in contrast to another set of ordinances and statutes, called casuistic laws, about which more will be said later.

The first four of the Ten Words deal in one way or another with the worship of God (Exodus 20:1-11). The people were to have no other God than YHWH. They were not to make any idols. They were to worship only the LORD. The Hebrew term translated as *worship* also means "serve" and is the same word used to describe Israel's service to Pharaoh. In other words, the people were to have no human master; they were to serve/worship only the LORD God (Exodus 20:3-5). They were reminded that God was zealous, punishing the disobedient but showing steadfast love to the faithful (Exodus 20:5-7). The longest of the first four stipulations dealt with keeping the Sabbath day of rest in remembrance of God's rest at the conclusion of the creation of the world (Exodus 20:8-11; Genesis 2:2-3; but see Deuteronomy 5:15).

The following six commandments deal with the relationships that were expected to exist within the community. Honor and care was to be extended to aging parents (Exodus 20:12). Murder, adultery, stealing, false witness, and coveting were forbidden (Exodus 20:13-17). These breaches in the social order were considered significantly harmful so as to require capital punishment. It is interesting, therefore, when instructions about appropriate punishment of thievery do not suggest such dire punishment (Exodus 22:1-4). It is possible that originally the commandment about stealing was referring to kidnapping, which was, in fact, defined as a capital offense (Exodus 20:15; see 21:16; Deuteronomy 24:7). The covenant cannot be maintained if these stipulations are ignored.

Covenant Stipulations: The Covenant Code

There is another set of statutes and ordinances, which scholars have entitled the "Covenant Code" or the "Book of the Covenant" (Exodus 20:22–23:19; 24:7). Both the Ten Words and the Covenant Code interrupt the narrative that begins in chapter nineteen and ends in chapter twenty-four. Both fulfill the function of providing the section on stipulations that is usually found in suzerain treaties/covenants, the civil model from which this spiritual metaphor is drawn.

The Book of the Covenant consists of a mixture of instructions that generally take a casuistic form. A basic law is stated, then various exceptions, with alternative actions, are listed. Rules concern the making of idols and the construction of altars, for instance (Exodus 20:23-26), or ordinances dealing with Hebrew slaves (Exodus 21:2-6). The topics range from property to appropriate forms of restitution in various circumstances (Exodus 21:28-36; 22:1-15). In some places it seems that an attempt has been made to clarify some of the Ten Commandments (Exodus 21:12-27). These examples illustrate the content and style of the Covenant Code. It is significant that many of these ordinances and statutes assume that Israel lives as a settled, agricultural people. These stipulations seem quite old, but they are appropriate only after the people have entered Canaan and are no longer a people wandering in the wilderness.

Moses Enters the Cloud

After the covenant was confirmed by sacrifice and sacral meal (Exodus 24:1-14), Moses again ascended the Mount Sinai. The "glory of the LORD" had "settled" on the mountain. After six days, on the seventh, God called to Moses; and Moses entered the dense cloud that enclosed the divine "glory" (Exodus 24:15-16, NRSV; see also Exodus 19:16, 20). God's "glory" (in Hebrew, *kabod*), in one of the major theological traditions of Israel, the priestly tradition, represented the very presence of God. It was a luminous light like "a blazing fire" (Exodus 24:17). The glory "settled" (in Hebrew, *shaken*) on the mountain but was impermanent; it did not abide or reside there (Exodus 24:16). For "forty days and forty nights," Moses stayed in the cloud in the presence of the Holy One (Exodus 24:18).

When Moses emerged from the cloud, he had the "two tablets of the covenant, tablets of stone, written with the finger of God" (Exodus 31:18, NRSV). But he also had much more: detailed instructions for the construction of a "tabernacle" (NRSV and NIV) and a guide for the ordination of priests and the conduct of sacrifices. The tabernacle was to be built with freewill offerings from the people (Exodus 25:2-7) to provide a place for God to *shaken* ("tent" or "tabernacle"; to "dwell" temporarily) with the people when they were not on the move (Exodus 25:8). There was also to be a moveable shrine or "ark" (not the same Hebrew word as used for Noah's ark; "chest" in the CEB and NIV) richly overlaid with gold and fitted with poles for its transport (Exodus 25:10-15). The tablets of the covenant that God made with the people were to be placed in the ark, thus providing its name, the Ark of the Covenant (Exodus 25:16, 21-22, NRSV).

Instructions were also given for the sanctuary furniture that was to be placed in the tabernacle (Exodus 25:23-40) as well as a detailed plan for the tabernacle itself (Exodus 26:1-27:21). The vestments for the priests, the ordination of the priests, the types of daily offerings, and other pertinent instructions are reported (Exodus 28:1–31:11). When the whole plan is considered carefully, the tabernacle sounds a great deal like the temple of Solomon that was constructed in the tenth century B.C. in Jerusalem (1 Kings 6:1-36; 7:13-51).

The final word Moses reports from the LORD concerns the Sabbath. As in the Ten Words, the people are told to sanctify the seventh day as a day of solemn rest honoring the God of creation, who in six days made "the heavens and earth, and on the seventh day the LORD rested" (Exodus 31:15, 17). Sabbath observance "in every generation" was to stand as a "covenant for all time" (Exodus 31:16), as a "sign forever" between God and the people of Israel (Exodus 31:17).

Most of the instructions that Moses reported receiving from God in the cloud were about the physical construction and ordering of the tabernacle with its personnel, a space and its functionaries, which were to be holy to God. But it is worth noting that the report concluded with a renewed emphasis, a strong admonition, concerning the sanctifying of the Sabbath. Sabbath is something people can observe wherever in the world they are. They don't need a temple or a king or even a movable shrine. All they need is an awareness of time. With this reminder, Moses underscored a most important point. God had not only directed the people with the Ten Commandments and the Book of the Covenant about how to live day by day, but the LORD had also claimed their time—all of their time— as well. Both our space and our time belong to God.

Live the Story

What does it mean for you that God made a covenant with God's people? If you are a Christian, you are in the same covenantal relationship as were the people of ancient Israel. In Jesus Christ, God's covenant has been extended to all. How can you show your acceptance of God's gracious establishment of such a wondrous relationship?

First of all, how well do you know the history of your deliverance, your redemption? Do you know it well enough to explain it to others? If not, how might you go about learning what God has, in fact, done for you? Are there persons you respect whom you can talk to? Do you know of the wide variety of theological and biblical resources likely to be found in your church library, public library, or on the Internet? What do your friends have to share? All of these questions are intended to suggest ways that you might begin to understand and rejoice in the covenant God has established.

Second, are there areas in your life that you find "judged" when you consider the Ten Commandments or the stipulations in the Covenant Code? If there are, you are not alone. The question is: What are you going to do about it? Do you find yourself fretting over what your neighbor has that you do not? Do you find it difficult to resist cheating a little on your taxes? How faithfully do you observe the Sabbath? The stipulations of the covenant are not intended to depress or demean you. They are aimed at helping you realize what is actually important in life and guiding you to enjoy life more fully.

Finally, how much do you want to have God in your life? Some people think that they want a close connection until it begins to happen. Are you prepared to have your values examined in the light of God's expectations? Are you able and willing to make changes? Can you take the criticism of others who want to help you grow in Christian discipleship? All of these things are necessary if you are to participate as fully as God wants you to in covenantal life. Is it worth it? Those who have tried it consistently give an unqualified "yes" to the question.

4.

Disobedience and Forgiveness

Exodus 32:1–40:38

Claim Your Story

Have you ever made a mistake? Called a wrong number on the phone? Turned the wrong way down a one-way street? Added incorrectly in your check book, leading you to overdraw? Introduced someone by the wrong name? Most of us have made such mistakes. Mistakes are easily forgiven.

Disobedience, however, is another matter. Have you ever purposely dialed a wrong number just to be a nuisance? Have you ever deliberately violated traffic laws? Have you ever knowingly written a bad check? Have you ever attempted to deceive someone by using an alias? If you have, then you have disobeyed the rules that govern our common life. Disobedience—particularly a serious act of disobedience—is more difficult to remedy. It is harder for someone else to forgive something done deliberately, and it can be a problem for the one who has been disobedient to deal with as well.

How do you tell the difference between making a mistake and being disobedient? Have you ever explained the fact that you were speeding at thirty-five miles an hour as a mistake in simply not recognizing that you were in a twenty-five-mile-an-hour zone? Does such a mistake make you less guilty of disobedience? Have you ever justified parking in a no-parking zone on the basis that you were going to be there only a short time? It is still illegal, and you have disobeyed the law. Would it make a difference if you had parked there because a person in your car needed immediate medical attention, and you had stopped to call 9-1-1? Probably, although it is still illegal. Have you ever cheated on your tax return? That is illegal.

On your marriage partner? That may not be illegal, but it is immoral—a form of religious disobedience—in the eyes of most Christians.

How do you make amends when you have made a mistake or been disobedient? Do you apologize? That will help. Do you change your behavior? That certainly can make a difference. Can you make another person overlook your mistake or forgive your disobedience? No, you can't; and that is what this incredible part of Exodus is all about.

Enter the Bible Story

The flow of the narrative of Exodus is dramatically broken by chapters 32–34. What should have followed the instructions on how to construct and outfit the tabernacle—logically speaking—was the description of the carrying out of those instructions; but that is not found until chapters 35–40. Instead, what follows is the report of a most severe case of disobedience, a total disregard for the covenantal stipulations we call the Ten Commandments. This is a story of transgression, forgiveness, and God's continuing gracious presence.

The People Violate the Covenant

The people had seen Moses enter the cloud that shrouded the top of Mount Sinai (Exodus 24:17-18) and waited and waited for Moses to return. As the days passed by, they grew anxious. Since they feared that Moses had abandoned them, they came to Aaron to ask that he "make gods" who would "go before" them, leading and protecting them, assuring them of the divine presence (Exodus 32:1, NRSV).

Unexpectedly, Aaron immediately complied. He had the people bring gold ornaments, melted them, and produced a golden calf (Exodus 32:2-4). Later in the passage, Aaron tells Moses that he simply threw the gold in the fire and the calf just emerged (Exodus 32:24). Whatever the exact nature of Aaron's complicity, an idol was presented to the people and they worshiped it (Exodus 32:4, 8). It is debated whether the golden calf was thought to be a representation of God—in Canaanite religion the bull is a symbol of Baal—or whether it was thought to represent a pedestal on which the invisible God of Israel stood. However it might be interpreted, in the mind of the people, it seems that a piece of metal, a golden trinket, was thought to assure the presence of the LORD. They had purposely—no mistake here—turned aside. They had disobeyed at a very basic level. They ignored God's commandments: "You must have no other gods before me. Do not make an idol for yourself....Do not bow down to them or worship them" (Exodus 20:3-5).

God's reaction was immediate and very negative. God told Moses to return to "your people," God no longer claimed them (Exodus 32:7). Israel had been "quick to turn aside from the way" God had commanded. They were "stiff-necked" (Exodus 32:8-9, NRSV). God expected the covenant stipulations to be kept. Because of the people's disobedience, God was prepared to abandon the people completely and work through Moses to "make a great nation." The people deserved severe punishment, and God was prepared for the divine wrath "to burn and devour them" (Exodus 32:9-10).

Moses Intercedes for the People

Moses immediately became an intercessor for Israel. The narrator makes this clear with the choice of the pronoun *your*. Moses insisted to God that the people were still "your own," that is, God's, people (Exodus 32:11). Moses then appealed for divine mercy on two accounts. First, Moses pointed out that the Egyptians would gloat. They would claim that God had brought the people out into the wilderness for the purpose of killing them; that was a claim God would not want the Egyptians to be able to make (Exodus 32:12). Second, Moses reminded God of the promises to Abraham, Isaac, and Jacob/Israel. These were the reason God had decided to deliver Israel from Egypt in the first place (Exodus 32:13; see 2:24; 3:6, 16-18; 6:5-8).

Then an amazing observation is given in a very matter-of-fact manner. The narrator tells us that, in response to Moses, "the LORD changed his mind about the terrible things he said he would do to his people" (Exodus 32:14). There is no question that punishment was justified. It would not have been unfair to hold the people accountable. But the simple statement that "the LORD changed his mind" is most remarkable—and for some people, most difficult to accept. That God can have such freedom challenges some who claim that God is immutable, unchangeable. Scripture offers a different view. When God considers it appropriate, God can and will change plans, particularly on an issue of forgiveness.

When Moses returned to camp and saw the revelry of the people, he cast down the tablets of the covenant, which he had brought down from the mountain, breaking them into pieces (Exodus 32:15-16, 19). He pulverized the golden calf and made the people drink water sprinkled with the golden dust (Exodus 32:20). Moses ordered the sons of Levi to execute those most deeply involved, some three thousand people (Exodus 32:26-28). By doing so, the Levites demonstrated their worthiness for the "service of the LORD" and became the core priestly group attending the tabernacle (Exodus 32:29, NRSV).

Moses then redressed the people, saying, "You have sinned a great sin. But now I will go up to the LORD; perhaps I can make atonement for your sin" (Exodus 32:30, NRSV). Despite the seriousness of their disobedience in making "gods of gold," Moses pled for divine forgiveness. Moses went so far as to tell God that he too wanted to be blotted out "of the scroll that you've written" if God was unwilling to forgive their sin (Exodus 32:31-32). God was not prepared to blot Moses out, but God did reserve the right to punish later any and all who might sin against God (Exodus 32:33-34).

The Question of God's Accompaniment

God ordered Moses and the people to leave Sinai/Horeb. They were to go to the land God had promised the forebears (33:1). But because they were "stubborn," God did not plan to accompany them (Exodus 33:2-3). When the people heard this, they went into mourning in hopes that God would reconsider (Exodus 33:4-6). Moses again challenged God. Moses wanted God to go with them and to make his intention to do so clear to the people (Exodus 33:12-13). Moses wanted assurance himself because it was only in that way that the people would recognized that God's favor was with Moses (Exodus 33:15-16). Indeed, Moses wanted to see God's "glory" (in Hebrew, *kabod*), the luminescence of the very presence of God (Exodus 33:18, NRSV).

Moses was not allowed to see God's glory, for no one was able to see God's face and live (Exodus 33:20; but see 24:1-11). Nonetheless, as confirmation that God would accompany Moses and the people on their trek toward Canaan, God said to Moses, "I will make all my goodness pass before you, and will proclaim before you the name, 'The LORD'; and I will be gracious to whom I will be gracious, and will show mercy on whom I will show mercy" (Exodus 33:19, NRSV). Then, after placing Moses in "a gap in the rock," God passed by, allowing Moses to see only his back (Exodus 33:22). Then something even more astounding took place. Moses was instructed to prepare a new set of stones, ascend Mount Sinai once again, and there receive a new set of tablets to replace those he had earlier smashed (Exodus 34:1-4).

At this point in the narrative, a truly extraordinary sketch of God's character appears. In a brief poetic utterance, we read: "The LORD, the LORD, a God merciful and gracious, slow to anger, and abounding in steadfast love and faithfulness, keeping steadfast love for the thousandth generation, forgiving iniquity and transgression and sin, yet by no means clearing the guilty, but visiting the iniquity of the parents upon the children and the children's children, to the third and the fourth generation" (Exodus 34:6-7, NRSV). This statement is a beautiful, succinct testimony describing the manner in which God engages humankind in relationship. It is a reflection on the wonder of God whose presence has and will accompany Moses and the people wherever they go.

About the Scripture

God's Graciousness Described

The importance of this declaration concerning the Lord God, whose name YHWH is twice repeated, is indicated in that it is repeated in whole or in part in the Old Testament in at least ten other passages (Numbers 14:18; 2 Chronicles 30:9; Nehemiah 9:17; Psalm 86:15; 103:8; 145:8; Jeremiah 32:18; Joel 2:13; Jonah 4:2; and Nahum 1:3). With seven terms, God's graciousness is cataloged: *merciful, gracious, slow to anger, abounding in steadfast love, faithfulness, keeping steadfast love, and forgiving.* Each of these terms strengthens or reinforces the cumulative impression of divine grace surpassing all expectations. Certainly, this understanding of God is underscored in the person of Jesus of Nazareth!

The Covenant Renewed

The beautiful statement just considered may well have been used in ritual settings for generations, but its first literary setting here in Exodus comes in response to the failure of the people to maintain the covenant. They had participated in the creation and worship of a bull image and deserved God's severe reprimand. At this point in the narrative, Moses asks once again for God's forgiveness (Exodus 34:8-9). God's answer to Moses' prayer was as gracious as Moses had hoped. God once again vowed to do wondrous things with Israel in order that all peoples might see and recognize God's special relationship with Israel. Israel was to be God's covenant partner and was promised a land, a place in the hill country of what has come to be called Palestine (Exodus·34:10-11). Israel, on her part, was not to enter into any treaties or covenants with any of the peoples of that land lest they and their religious practices "become a dangerous trap" (Exodus 34:11-13). There were to be no more golden calves.

As with the formation of the covenant in the first instance, in chapters 19–24, here too another set of stipulations is recorded in connection with the renewal of the covenant. These commandments deal with various ritual practices. They are primarily suited for the agricultural setting the people will know in the land of Canaan. There are instructions concerning the festival of unleavened bread (Exodus 34:18); the Sabbath (Exodus 34:21); and the festivals of weeks, first fruits, and ingathering (Exodus 34:22). Guidance is given for the sacrifices of redemption of the firstborn and first fruits (Exodus 34:19-20, 25-26). These stipulations clearly assume that the people are in Canaan and not in the wilderness. They are nonetheless quite old and; while they did not replace the Ten Commandments, they were considered sufficiently worthy for preservation that they were recorded at this significant place in Israel's story.

Moses' Special Relationship With God

As the story of Exodus has developed, it has become clear that Moses had a very special relationship with God. At the conclusion of chapter thirty-four this connection is dramatically demonstrated. When Moses came down from the mountain, the fact that he had been in the presence of the divine was evident: his face shone (Exodus 34:29, 35). To relieve the discomfort this apparently caused his people, Moses wore a veil. When he went into the tent of meeting, he removed the veil but put it on again when he came out (Exodus 34:33-35). Perhaps this was a result of being in the presence of God, the effect of the bright glow of God's "glory" on Moses' face, but the text does not really explain the phenomenon.

What is worth noting is that, from the beginning of Exodus to the end, the issue of divine presence was of deep concern. God assured Moses that God would be with him before Moses ever confronted Pharaoh (Exodus 3:12; 4:12). The people had worried in the wilderness about God's presence (Exodus 17:7). From the time when God's "glory" (*kabod*), veiled by the heavy cloud, had settled on Mount Sinai, Moses and the people had struggled with a desire for and fear of the presence of God (Exodus 24:15). After the debacle of the golden calf, Moses was deeply concerned whether God would go with him and the people and had to be reassured by God (Exodus 32:14). Once again, Moses had prayed for God's presence even after receiving the proclamation of God name (Exodus 34:9, NRSV). Now Moses' shining face was the eloquent demonstration of God's continuing presence.

A second noteworthy observation is that Moses was known as one with whom God spoke "face to face, as one speaks to a friend" (Exodus 33:11, NRSV). We are told practically nothing about the appearance of God, but we do learn that God communicated with Moses. God is said to have repeatedly talked with Moses (Exodus 34:29, 32, 34-35). Whenever that occurred, Moses' face would glow. Moses, in turn, talked with the people on God's behalf (Exodus 34:31-34). Moses was unmatched as an intercessor for the people and a spokesman for God. God was indeed with Moses.

The Completion of the Work

Following the renewal of the covenant, Moses called the people together for further instructions, with a special reminder of the sanctity of the Sabbath (Exodus 35:1-3). They were put to work carefully carrying out all of the instructions Moses had given them (see chapters 25–31) for constructing the various parts of the Tabernacle and its furnishings, and for preparations for the priestly personnel. This whole project is reported in detail (Exodus 35:4–39:42). How many hands and how many hours were involved is not reported, but it was a major job. Moses, conspicuously absent in the narrative during all the work, reappears when it is completed to give his approval: "When Moses saw that they in fact had done all the work exactly as the LORD had commanded, Moses blessed them" (Exodus 39:43).

All that remained was for the tabernacle to be erected. This was to be done by Moses "on the first day of the first month"—on New Year's Day—in the second year of their travels in the wilderness (Exodus 40:1, 17). Moses was told to perform a series of actions intended to sanctify the tabernacle and its personnel (Exodus 40:9-14). And as surely expected, Moses "did everything exactly as the LORD had commanded him" (Exodus 40:16). Seven times more during the report this repetitious summary is repeated; seven times all was done "as the LORD commanded Moses" (Exodus 40:19, 21, 23, 25, 27, 29, 32). This report has the sound of a liturgical incantation, and perhaps it served such a function each time the consecration of the tabernacle was celebrated. The tabernacle was carefully erected and each part carefully placed. Then we are told, "Moses had finished all the work" (Exodus 40:33).

The Cloud and the Glory

After the work was done, Moses and the people waited to see what would happen. All along, their concern was whether God would in fact accompany them as their journey continued. Then the text reports, "the cloud covered the tent of meeting (in Hebrew, 'ohel mo'ed), and the glory filled the tabernacle (in Hebrew, mishkan)" (Exodus 40:34, NRSV). The cloud was that special cloud that had affirmed, while hiding, the splendor of God's presence, God's glory, on Mount Sinai. Because it "settled" (shaken) on the "tent of meeting" and because "the glory of the LORD filled the tabernacle," Moses could not enter (Exodus 40:35, NRSV). In these two verses (Exodus 40:34-35), a tradition largely lost about a "tent of meeting" (Exodus 33:7-11) has been brought together with the narrative about the tabernacle so that the two have come to be understood as one and the same (Exodus 40:38).

With this brief note—almost a postscript—the presence of God is assured. Whenever the cloud was "taken up," the people knew that God was moving on to another place and that they too were to move. When the cloud remained over the tabernacle, God's presence, God's glory, was there and the people stayed in place (Exodus 40:36-37). Because the tabernacle was built to be transportable, the people realized from the beginning that God did not need nor intend to stay rooted in any one particular geographic place. The Book of Exodus concludes with these words: "For the cloud of the LORD was on the tabernacle by day, and the fire was in the cloud by night, before the eyes of all the house of Israel at each stage of their journey" (Exodus 40:38, NRSV). God's presence went with Moses and God's people.

Live the Story

What does it take to be willing to forgive someone for committing a grave offense? Have you ever had to try to do so? Can the sin or the violation simply be forgotten? Should it be? How can anyone learn from the incident if it is glossed over and left unaddressed? Is that what God did? How can we benefit from reflecting on this event in Exodus?

Well, our passage suggests that we need to own up to our own actions. We have to understand clearly how our actions have offended others and are displeasing to God. Have you considered your own behavior lately? Have you broken a confidence or proven untrustworthy? Have you purposely ignored another or spread a rumor? How do you think others might feel about that? Have you begun to "worship" objects or values that are contrary to God's way? Do you think that such things matter to God? What should you do?

Until there is understanding that one has transgressed against another, there can be no change of behavior, no "repentance." Remember that it is not easy for someone to forgive another, so don't think that a simple "I'm sorry" will automatically set things right. Nonetheless, the repair of a breach in relationship can begin only as we reach out to one another and to God in repentance. God assures us that we will have the divine presence with us as we try. Are you ready to begin? God is willing to help.

5.

Approaching God in Purity

Leviticus 1:1–16:34

Claim Your Story

Have you ever thought much about what it means to say that something is "sacred"? Do you talk about things at church that are sacred? The Bible? The bread and the wine? The sanctuary? Or do you use the term *sacred* mainly with regard to things that our nation holds as sacred? Our constitution? Our flag? Lives given in defense of our country? Do you even use the term *sacred* at all? Isn't the term rather quaint and old fashioned?

If you have ever set something apart as particularly special, then you are treating it as something sacred. That's what the word means: something that is reserved for special, not common, use. What are some things like that in your life? A special book that your grandfather gave you? The last letter you received from a dying friend? A photograph from your childhood? The rocking chair you used when you were nursing your children? A coin you found on your sixteenth birthday? Any number of things can be set apart because of the memories they recall or because of relationships they represent. They become sacred to us.

Are there special ways you handle things you consider as sacred? Are there particular times and places where these sacred things are brought out for others to see or touch? Do you talk about your sacred things, or are they secret, known only to you? Do you know of things that others hold as sacred? Do they seem strange to you? Why do things that we honor as sacred sometimes seem weird to those outside our circle? What does it mean to decide to consider something sacred? How does that affect our attitude toward the sacred object and toward any who do not relate to our sacred things as we do?

Leviticus is a book about sacred things, holy things. Few people read the Book of Leviticus regularly today. Many find it strange when they do. Try to keep in mind all of the questions just asked about things sacred as you consider Leviticus so that the book may make more sense to you.

Enter the Bible Story

Leviticus was so named because Aaron and his sons, Levites, are addressed directly in a few places (Leviticus 6:8, 24; 17:1; 21:1). For the most part, however, the people as a whole are the presumed audience. The instructions are intended to provide the members of the community, singly and collectively, with information on how to conduct the proper worship of God, how to order life before the sacred presence of God. Leviticus is at the center of the Pentateuch (or the Torah, the first five books of the Old Testament) and, in the narrative, expands greatly the significance of the people's stay at Mount Sinai.

About the Scripture

Two Perspectives on Holiness

The Book of Leviticus (known in Hebrew tradition as *vayikra'*, "and He said," from 1:1) is comprised of two major sources of tradition, each of which dealing with priestly concerns. The first is known by scholars as the Priestly Code and includes Leviticus 1–16. The second is known as the Holiness Code, found in Leviticus 17–26. An appendix, Leviticus 27, elaborates on some of the material in the Holiness Code. Each of the two major sources uses distinct vocabulary and has a different overall theme. For the Priestly Code, the primary concern is the sacredness of the tabernacle and its personnel. The pollution of the sacred occurs because of Israel's moral and ritual laxity. For the Holiness Code, holiness is not limited to the tabernacle. The land as a whole—and all who dwell in it—is thought to be the place where holiness is found and to be protected. Pollution is not mainly caused by ritual violations but, rather, is the result of Israel's violations of the covenant.

Offerings of Thanksgiving

The sacrificial system in ancient Israel was basic to remembering, celebrating, and maintaining Israel's relationship with God. In Leviticus, the offerings of animals and birds are presented at the tabernacle. Later, the Temple in Jerusalem serves as the place of sacrificial offerings. After the Temple was destroyed in A.D. 70, prayer replaced animal sacrifice as the avenue for communion with God. Most Christians and Jews today offer sacrifices only symbolically through gifts of money and through prayer.

Several categories of sacrifices are described in Leviticus. The most costly was the entirely burnt offering of a bull (Leviticus 1:3-9). It could function as an offering of thanksgiving or a sacrifice seeking atonement or expiation. A bull, "male without blemish," was slaughtered and offered up to God, totally consumed by fire on the altar. In some instances, a sheep, a goat, or even a dove or pigeon could serve as a entirely burnt offering (Leviticus 1:10-17, NRSV). In every case, the animal or bird was totally cremated as "an entirely burned offering, a food gift of soothing smell to the LORD" (Leviticus 1:9, 13, 17). A second form of the entirely burnt offering involved the sacrifice of grain. Coarse grain or goods made from grain could be offered. The sacrifice would be totally consumed by the altar fire (Leviticus 2:1-16). Detailed instructions for the proper carrying out of these sacrifices were given to the priests (Leviticus 6:23).

A third form of sacrifice was the sacrifice of well-being or the peace offering (Leviticus 3:1-17). This type of offering was made generally as an act of thanksgiving. It differed from the entirely burnt sacrifices in that only the fatty portion of the animal was turned "into smoke on the altar as a food offering by fire" (Leviticus 3:5, 11, 16, NRSV). Israel was forbidden to eat any fat or blood for all generations (Leviticus 3:17). The rituals associated with the offering of well-being were carefully recorded (Leviticus 7:11-36).

Although animal/bird sacrifice may seem primitive and somewhat repulsive to many contemporary Christians and Jews, the purpose behind such acts need not be. To acknowledge dependence upon God or to express gratitude for divine care and guidance was the intention, and that kind of "sacrifice" remains appropriate today.

Purification and Reparation Offerings

An allowance was made for the effects of unintentional transgression. Whether a priest (Leviticus 4:3-12), the community as a whole (Leviticus 4:13-21), a ruler (Leviticus 4:22-27), or simply an individual (Leviticus 4:27-35) inadvertently did something that violated God's commandments, atonement could be made (Leviticus 4:3, 21, 26, 31, 35). If someone who could do so failed to testify (Leviticus 5:1), if someone touched something unclean (Leviticus 5:2-3), or if someone uttered a rash oath (Leviticus 5:4), a guilt offering could be made to effect atonement (Leviticus 5:6, 10, 13). Public confession was expected (Leviticus 5:5). The worth of the sacrifices to be offered ran the scale from costly to relatively inexpensive—anyone who desired to do so could afford such an offering (Leviticus 5:7).

Likewise, if anyone were to commit a "trespass and sin unintentionally in any of the holy things of the LORD"—perhaps food dedicated to God was unintentionally eaten or some part of the tabernacle was accidentally damaged—a sin offering could be presented (Leviticus 5:15, NRSV). The monetary value of the animal to be sacrificed was to be calculated and a fifth more was to be added to pay for the damage done, then the sacrifice could be carried out (Leviticus 5:14-15). Rituals for the conduct of these sacrifices were included (Leviticus 6:24–7:10).

Not all transgression, however, is unintentional. Sometimes people deliberately violate God's way. They might lie to a neighbor about a deposit or pledge, they might steal, they might defraud, they might lie about something that they have found that belongs to another, or they might swear falsely (Leviticus 6:2-3). Please note: Any such offense against a neighbor was a trespass against the Lord (Leviticus 6:2). What then was to happen? If the guilty party acknowledged the wrongdoing, reparation could be made. The offended person was to receive one-hundred-twenty percent the value of the damage (if it could be determined) and a sacrificial animal of equal cost was to be brought to the priest for sacrifice. Then atonement may be made (Leviticus 6:5-7).

Obviously, mistakes can be made; deliberate transgressions occur. While any damage needs repair, those involved need not face permanent rejection by God or the community. The sacrificial rituals of ancient Israel enabled atonement and made reparation possible. As there was grace in the covenant God made with Israel at Mount Sinai, so there is also grace in the sacrificial system.

Aaron's Priesthood

In the midst of all of the ritual and cultic instructions so far considered, there is a pause. Those who were responsible for carrying out the sacrificial system were Aaron (Moses' elder brother) and his sons (Leviticus 8:1-2). Moses is described in detail, carrying out the instructions concerning the ordination of the priesthood (Leviticus 8:2-35; see Exodus 28:1–29:37). It is significant that Moses, who God spoke with "face to face" (Exodus 33:11; and Deuteronomy 34:10), takes the lead here. As important as the priesthood was to be, the place of the prophets, as represented by Moses, was equally or even more so. The details of the ritual are interesting, but in some places somewhat obscure. It is clear, though, that appropriate sacrifices were offered, the tabernacles were properly cleansed, and the priests were rightly ordained (Leviticus 8:6-29), all in the presence of the people (Leviticus 8:4-5). The newly consecrated priests, including Aaron, were charged to remain in the tabernacle for seven days, perhaps in order for the holiness of the place to set them apart adequately (Leviticus 8:31-35). Then "Aaron and his sons did everything the LORD commanded through Moses" (Leviticus 8:36).

Following their consecration, Aaron and his sons officiated for the first time over sacrifices in the tabernacle on behalf of the people (Leviticus 9:1-21). Aaron and Moses blessed the people (Leviticus 9:22-23). And to the wonder of the people, "the glory of the LORD appeared to all the people. Fire came out from the LORD and consumed the burnt offering and the fat on the altar" (Leviticus 9:23-24, NRSV). But at the height of what was clearly a marvelous moment, Nadab and Abihu, two of Aaron's sons, perhaps in over-exuberance or perhaps in ignorance, violated ritual law. Without authorization, they offered burning incense, "unholy fire," before God (Leviticus 10:1, NRSV; "unauthorized fire" in CEB and NIV). Rather than waiting for divine fire to light their censers, they lit them themselves, thereby disregarding the instruction to honor the sacredness of the altar and the tabernacle. Because of this transgression against the sacred, they were immediately consumed by divine fire (Leviticus 10:2). The issue had to do with distinguishing "between the holy and the common, and between the unclean and the clean" (Leviticus 10:10). Moses and Aaron exchanged angry words about how things were and were not done correctly, but the bottom line was that the action of God remained immediate and inscrutable (Leviticus 10:16-20).

From the perspective of contemporary Christians and Jews, these chapters are at best strange and at worst very disturbing. The punishment that fell on Nadab and Abihu seems utterly disproportionate to their offense. But what is illustrated by the story is a two-fold message: The holiness of God is to be taken with utmost seriousness. There is much we may not understand about the sacred and the holy, but we are reminded that God is God and we are not.

Rules for Maintaining Purity

The next five chapters of Leviticus describe four sources of impurity to be avoided. By following these rules, Israel demonstrates her distinctiveness in the world. Holiness and sacredness in the Bible have to do with being set apart for special service of some sort. To the degree that the people of Israel remain "clean" they are considered ritually "holy." These laws, for the most part, do not seem to allow any rational explanation from the standpoint of contemporary standards, but they have functioned well across the centuries to enable Jews to maintain their distinctiveness.

The first source of possible impurity comes from touching the flesh or blood of any creature designated as "unclean." The "clean" and "unclean" creatures are enumerated in chapter eleven. In chapter twelve, instructions are given for the purification of women after childbirth because of the presence of blood. A third source of possible uncleanness concerns touching persons who have any of a variety of skin diseases, which were relatively widespread in antiquity. These rules are set out in chapters thirteen and fourteen, with instruction for the priests, in terms of when and how people suffering such problems could be purified. Then finally, the fourth source of impurity, dealt with in chapter fifteen, deals with contact with various genital discharges. In each instance, means of purification are detailed. The issue is always how to maintain the purity of the tabernacle and the community as a whole; individuals were to be segregated, as necessary, in order that the tabernacle and people might maintain their holiness before God.

These statutes are strange to most contemporary Christians. These laws do not seem at all relevant to the lives we lead today. Perhaps, as already suggested, their primary value for most of us is that they are a stark reminder of the difference between the divine and the human. We do not—probably cannot—understand all of God's ways; but we are, nonetheless, called to live as much in harmony with divine instruction as possible. While we may never comprehend the reasons for some of these rules, we can trust that God's intention was and is for the good of God's people. We continue to live in faith.

The Day of Atonement

Chapter sixteen sets forth instructions for perhaps the most important ritual day in the Israelite/Jewish calendar, the Day of Atonement (in Hebrew, *Yom Kippur*). This day was to be observed "on the tenth day of the seventh month," that is, ten days after the fall new year (Leviticus 16:29; 23:27). The chapter begins by picking up the narrative from Leviticus 10:20, with the Lord directing Moses and Aaron on what needed to be done to purify the tabernacle after the death of Aaron's sons (Leviticus 16:1-2). Aaron is given instructions for the various rituals required to cleanse the tabernacle. Several different sacrifices were to be made, with the sacred blood of the slaughtered animals strategically placed. Aaron alone was to carry out these actions (Leviticus 16:3-19). But toward the end of the chapter there is a change of focus. Instructions are given for carrying out this festival in subsequent generations, long after the days of Aaron and Moses (Leviticus 16:32). Aaron began the festival in response to a ritual catastrophe, but its continuation expands its meaning.

Across the Testaments

Atonement

Atonement is a theological theme that spans both the Old and New Testaments. The issue is not one of appeasement; God does not need to be appeased. In Leviticus, the issue has to do with removing the barrier erected by sin that separates God's people from God. The high priest (initially Aaron) officiated in the supreme ritual of purification, namely the Day of Atonement. In the New Testament, the act of atonement was linked closely with the ministry and death/resurrection of Jesus (see Mark 10:45; 14:24; Romans 3:25). The Book of Hebrews draws heavily and explicitly on the description of the work of the high priest in relation to the Day of Atonement (see Hebrews 2:17; 4:14-15:10; 10:19-25).

Apart from the rituals and sacrifices intended for the purification of the tabernacle, the greater benefit for the people as a whole lies in the act of atonement made for the community. A goat was selected and brought to the priest, who in turn made confession for "all the iniquities of the people of Israel, and all their transgression, all their sins." These were then transferred to the goat (Leviticus 16:21, NRSV). The goat was taken out into the wilderness and released, thereby removing all the sins of the people from the tabernacle and the camp (Leviticus 16:22). What's more, this instruction was to "be an everlasting statute for you, to make atonement for the people of Israel once in the year for all their sins" (Leviticus 16:34, NRSV).

We might not understand all of the details of the rules about purity and impurity, but the need for atonement is real. In this festival, God's gracious care for God's people can be seen clearly. No matter what may have happened or what people may have done, at least once a year all transgression and sin was to be taken away; all the impurities that separated the people from the Holy One were purged, covered, expiated. People could begin anew, with the knowledge that they had been brought into the correct relationship with God, not by their doing but strictly on divine initiative. Atonement meant reconciliation and was the gift of God. For Christians, this work is considered completed in the life, death, and resurrection of Jesus Christ. Christians believe that Jesus Christ provides atonement for all.

Live the Story

How can one begin to understand and appreciate what these instructions might mean for daily living? Try setting some things apart in your kitchen or garage to be used at only a designated time. Perhaps you can decide that yellow squash cannot be placed in the same refrigerator drawer with zucchini? How could you rearrange your shelves? Or what if you decide that you will not prepare meat on the same grill that you use to make grilled-cheese sandwiches? Will you buy two grills? Or in the garage, try placing all of the screwdrivers and wrenches in a cabinet separate from all other tools. Will you need to add a cabinet? Try setting aside one particular hammer to be used only for hanging pictures. Do this for a week, and see how you feel about it.

Most Christians do not normally separate food, kitchen utensils, or tools in the ways suggested above; but if we did, we might begin to have some sense of what the ancient Israelites dealt with when trying to deal with the sacred. Some Jews and Muslims still observe food laws and have to plan their kitchens and cooking accordingly. It is difficult for many of us to imagine doing this, particularly when some of the categories of things set apart seem rather arbitrary.

Perhaps more to the point will be a consideration of what is important about regarding some things as sacred. What are some special places you think should be set apart for special use? For some, the sanctuary at church is such a place. For others, a particular spot in the garden or in your home may have that quality. What is it that makes you think of a certain place as special? Is it the furnishings? Is it the primary activity that goes on there? Is it a sense of tranquility? Any of these qualities may serve to make a place special, even "sacred." Do you make a place sacred by yourself? Do you need others to acknowledge such a place? Do you find guidance from the Bible or from custom or from cherished relatives or friends?

What might you do to stay close to God? What spiritual practices could help you continue to love God and neighbor? Offering personal prayer, including prayers of confession? Doing Bible study? Visiting jail or prison inmates? Singing hymns and songs of praise? Showing hospitality to the outsider? Keeping Sabbath? Living simply? Showing generosity to the poor? Partaking of the Lord's Supper? Standing up for justice?

6.

Sanctification
and the Holiness of God

Leviticus 17:1–27:34

Claim Your Story

Are there items in your home that have real monetary value, such as jade figurines or diamond jewelry or an iPad®? How is the value determined? Who sets a monetary figure for such items? Does the marketplace help in establishing value? How about something like a painting or a coin collection or an antique desk? Is the same process used? Is there more subjectivity involved? What is taken into consideration in establishing an estimate?

How do you feel about any of the items mentioned above that are in your possession? Do you take special care of them? Do you take out fire insurance? Have you installed an alarm system in your home to ward off burglary? Do you talk about these items with anyone or with only a few trusted friends and relatives? Do you take these items out to show them off? Many people never use their valuable silver or china for fear of it being tarnished or broken. Are these items still of worth? What makes something valuable to you?

Some items clearly have "street value." Silver and gold prices are determined in the commercial trading markets. The same can be said about some types of coins, antiques, art, and so forth. Other things have personal value because of family associations (grandmother's ring), individual interests (a train set from childhood), or the source of the item (a stone picked up during a vacation). All are valuable because you or someone else has placed worth on them.

While it is not absolutely the case, to a degree one can distinguish between something being "sacred" and something being "holy" in terms of how value is understood. "Sacred" items are set apart for special use and thereby derive their "sacredness." "Holy" items are declared intrinsically valuable by someone and are thereby set apart. According to the dictionary, "sacred" and "holy" mean the basically same thing—"set apart." But in Leviticus, a slight distinction is drawn between sacred rituals defined by God and relationships made holy by the divine presence.

Enter the Bible Story

As in the previous chapters of Leviticus (1–16), much seems strange to contemporary Christians in the Holiness Code (17–26) and the appendix (27). The landscape in these chapters is unfamiliar to most of us. Thus, we often skip past this material. Careful attention, however, does offer some surprising rewards. The people of Israel and their relationship with the Holy One, is the primary focus. We can learn from their experiences.

The Significance of Blood

Those of us who do not offer sacrifice (or slaughter the animals whose meat we eat) find the emphasis on blood in Leviticus hard to grasp. We really don't want to know about such things. "TMI" (too much information) is probably the response of many. Blood, however, is important; for blood and life are intimately connected. In ancient Israel, blood was considered the source of power for animals, including humans. Blood was not to be consumed (Leviticus 17:10, 12, 14), nor was spilled blood to be left uncovered (Leviticus 17:13). Blood, the life-source of all animals, was considered essential for sacrificial acts of atonement (Leviticus 17:13; see 16:14-15, 18, 27).

These words concerning the significance of blood are directly connected to a prohibition against slaughtering an animal outside the camp, without bringing the carcass to the priests (Leviticus 17:3-6). The point of this ordinance was to discourage participation in sacrifices to "goat-demons" that were apparently assumed important to the people (Leviticus 17:7; see also 19:26). Neither the Israelites nor any aliens in their midst were allowed to make sacrifice without coming before the priests (Leviticus 17:8-9, 13).

While we are not tempted to participate in sacrifices to "goat-demons," various practices and customs in our society can lead us away from God. Forms of nationalism or some business practices or over-emphasis on physical beauty or the accumulation of wealth as well as various other temptations may require our abstinence—and that is not easy. As with Israel, nonetheless, God directs us away from what will separate us from God and render us unholy.

Holy God, Holy People

The next three chapters of the Holiness Code are especially important. The basis for any discussion of holiness is lodged in one fact: The Lord God is holy. The people are called to participate in that holiness and are given explicit instructions based alone on the authority of the Lord: "I am the LORD your God" (Leviticus 18:2, 4-6, 21, 30; 19:3-4, 10, 12, 14, 16, 18, 25, 28, 30-32, 34, 36-37; 20:8). Because God is holy, so shall the people be holy (Leviticus 19:2). And because they are holy they are to seek to imitate God and live accordingly.

In Leviticus 19 is an interpretation and expansion of the Ten Commandments (see Exodus 20). But before looking at this material we should note the "envelope" which surrounds it. Chapters 18 and 20 provide an interesting context for the admonition to be holy like God. In chapter 17, the importance of blood was interpreted in the context of a warning against a form of pagan worship, sacrifice to "goat-demons" (Leviticus 17:7). In chapter 18, a long series of prohibited sexual behaviors is presented; and here too the admonitions come as a warning for the people not to participate in various activities common to the Egyptians, from whose land they have fled, and the Canaanites, into whose land they will enter (Leviticus 18:2-3, 24; 20:23). The penalty for disobedience is clear: expulsion from the land. As God cast out the Canaanites for their iniquity—"the land vomited out its inhabitants"—so would Israel be expelled from the land if they participated in the prohibited activities (18:24-28).

Although the biblical text does not make it explicit, most of the prohibited behaviors were likely somehow related to the religious practices of the Egyptians and Canaanites. Sexual acts in connection with the worship of fertility deities probably involved indiscriminate sexual contact with anyone present. They were sexual orgies; and before the Lord, they were perversions.

The Hebrew euphemism for sexual relationships was "to uncover the nakedness" of another. One might, in the throes of religious "ecstasy" of one of these orgies, have sex with a sister or brother or some other relative, a neighbor's wife or husband, relations with someone of the same gender, someone who was ritually "unclean," or even with a non-human animal (Leviticus 18:7-23). All such behavior was prohibited. These are rules against incest, but that was not their first importance. In this same context, the sacrifice of children to Molech—an act of "worship"—as well as contact with "mediums and wizards" are also condemned. It seems likely that all of these prohibitions were related in some way to pagan fertility worship practices (Leviticus 18:21; 20:2-5; see also 19:26-31). Some carried capital punishment as their penalty (Leviticus 20:2, 5, 9, 11-16), while others brought banishment from the community or childlessness (20:17-21).

Chapters 18 and 20 form the context for the explicit instructions about how God expects the people to "be holy" (Leviticus 19:2; 20:6). By doing as directed, the people will live (Leviticus 18:5). Ritual guidelines are to be followed (Leviticus 19:5-8). The poor are to be considered when reaping the fields (Leviticus 19:9-10). The Ten Commandments that deal with intra-community relationships are underscored and elaborated on (Leviticus 19:11-16, 32, 35-36). There are instructions about agriculture and the treatment of slaves (Leviticus 19:19-25). In the midst of these instructions is a basic "rule" that will come to provide a shorthand summary of all of these laws: "You must not hate your fellow Israelite in your heart. Rebuke your fellow Israelite strongly so you don't become responsible for his sin. You must not take revenge nor hold a grudge against any of your people; instead you must love your neighbor as yourself; I am the LORD" (Leviticus 19:17-18: see also 19:34). Not hating another, offering correction when necessary, and loving others as oneself are at the heart of all of the actions that enable a person to move toward being holy as God is holy.

Love Your Neighbor as Yourself

In Leviticus, the instruction to love one's neighbor as one's self is lodged in a context aimed at erasing hatred and vengeance (Leviticus 19:18). In the New Testament, Jesus is remembered as referring to this verse when asked what one must do to have life everlasting, connecting it also with the commandment to love God alone (Matthew 19:16-22; Mark 12:28-34; Luke 10:25-38). Paul also used Leviticus 19:18 in his instructions to the congregation at Rome, urging them to owe no one anything but love, noting that love "doesn't do anything wrong to a neighbor; therefore love is what fulfills the Law" (Romans 13:8-10; see also Galatians 5:14).

Holy Priests, Holy Offerings, Holy Days

Special rules applied to those who became priests. As those who performed sacrifices to God on behalf of the community, the priests had to avoid defilement. That meant, for instance, that they could participate in the burial rites of only their closest blood relatives—not even of the wife of a priest—and they were not allowed to follow mourning customs such as shaving their heads or beards (Leviticus 21:1-6, 10-12). Their wives were to be of good reputation (Leviticus 21:7-8, 14-15). A daughter of a priest who profaned herself through prostitution was to be put to death (Leviticus 21:9). None of the sons of Aaron (that is, the priesthood) who had a "blemish" (was blind, lame, mutilated; had broken bones) could serve at the altar. The "blemished" ones could still eat from the offerings dedicated to the priests, but they were not eligible to function as priests (Leviticus 21:16-24). Special instructions concerned who could and who could not partake of the donations made for the care of the priests and for the need for purification for all who did partake (Leviticus 22:1-16). Included are detailed ordinances about who could present an offering in payment of a vow or as a freewill offering and the quality (no blemishes) of the sacrificial animals (Leviticus 22:17-30; see also the appendix in 27:1-33).

The Lord also directed Moses to speak to the people about the weekly Sabbath and the appointed festivals that were to be convened annually.

This festival calendar, found in several other places but with slight varia-tions, was rooted deeply in Israel's historical memory (Leviticus 23:4-44; see also Exodus 23:10-19; 34:18-24; Numbers 28:9-31; Deuteronomy 16:1-17). There are six annual festivals. Passover and Unleavened Bread, originally separate, came to be interconnected after Israel entered Canaan and were held "in the first month" on the fourteenth and fifteenth day. This came to be understood as the first day of the liturgical calendar. This combined festival remembered the exodus from Egypt and the eating of unleavened bread (Leviticus 23:4-8). The second festival was that of the offering of the First Fruits, which took place immediately after Passover and commemorated the first spring harvest (Leviticus 23:11). The third festival was the Festival of Weeks (known in Christian tradition as Pentecost). It came fifty days after First Fruits and was also a celebration of harvest. The fourth, fifth, and sixth festivals all come near one another in the seventh month. The Festival of Trumpets is on the first day (Leviticus 23:23-25), the Day of Atonement is on the tenth (Leviticus 23:26-32), and then the Festival of Booths begins on the fifteenth day and lasts for seven days (Leviticus 23:33-36). These last three mark the beginning of the New Year in the civil calen-dar as well as the beginning of the agricultural year. The festivals con-centrate on a time of reflection and repentance, and prayers for winter rains so necessary for the crops in the coming year.

The materials in the chapters we have been considering are not of utmost interest to contemporary Christians. However, they once again underscore the importance of the lifestyle expected of God's covenant people. Israel was set apart as a holy people by a holy God and was commanded to live accordingly. We do not need to adopt all of ancient Israel's institutions and practices, but we should take seriously the challenge to live lives that bring honor to God's name.

The Sabbatical Year and the Year of Jubilee

As the Holiness Code draws near its conclusion, two very interesting observances are noted, a Sabbatical Year and a Jubilee Year. The first, the Sabbatical Year, was designed to give the land a periodic rest every six years. The whole land—the fields and the vineyards—was to be left fallow;

there was to be a complete rest for the land (Leviticus 25:3-4). While the people and animals were allowed to eat what the land naturally brought forth, they were not to plant or reap (Leviticus 25:6-7). Contemporary farmers know the importance of crop rotation. In Leviticus, however, this observance was not only a means by which to preserve the land from being worn out. It was also a religious observance that emphasized the people's ongoing dependence and reliance upon God.

The Jubilee Year had a more involved purpose. Every fifty years, "on the tenth day of the seventh month—on the day of atonement—you shall have the trumpet sounded throughout all your land. And you shall hallow the fiftieth year and you shall proclaim liberty throughout the land to all its inhabitants" (Leviticus 25:9-10, NRSV). This was the Jubilee Year.

As with the Sabbatical Year, the land was to be given a total rest (Leviticus 25:11). The crops of the year preceding the Jubilee would be sufficient to feed the population during the Jubilee (Leviticus 25:18-22). But it was more than just a rest for the land, for everyone was to return to the property that by heredity belonged to their family (Leviticus 25:10). The implications of this were profound. To make it possible for everyone to be able to return to their original homesteads, all indebtedness had to be removed. Thus, every fifty years the economic structures of the community were to be adjusted so that there would be no debts or capital loans, neither poverty nor great financial inequity.

Allowances were made to enable the system to work fairly. When a sale of property was made, the length of time to the jubilee year was factored in to determine a fair price (Leviticus 25:13-17). No land was to be sold in perpetuity, since all the land belonged to God. From the divine standpoint, the people of Israel were as "immigrants and foreign guests" (Leviticus 25:23). Thus, there was to be a system for redemption of land in order to return it to the original family owners (Leviticus 25:24-28).

There were several prohibitions. Property within a walled community could pass in perpetuity to a purchaser if not redeemed within a year, but neither the houses in open land nor the land could be sold in perpetuity (Leviticus 25:29-31, 34). Interest-bearing loans could not be made by one Israelite to another (Leviticus 25:35-38). Nor could any Israelite take another Israelite as a slave in payment of debt; they were to be considered hired laborers and treated accordingly (Leviticus 25:39-43). If an Israelite became enslaved to a non-Israelite, he was to be redeemed by a close male relative—called the "redeemer" (in Hebrew, *go'el*)—at a price fairly determined in terms of the closeness of the Jubilee (Leviticus 25:47-53). Nonetheless, if his redemption was not accomplished before the Jubilee, then he was to be released from his service (Leviticus 25:54-55). It is not clear in terms of historical evidence whether the Jubilee was ever actually celebrated, but it certainly served as a grand statement concerning how the holy people of the holy God were to order their life together.

About the Scripture

Redeemer and Redemption

The term *redeemer* (in Hebrew, *go'el*) is important in the Bible. If a relative was enslaved by indebtedness or in some other way had lost his property, a close male relative was designated as the "redeemer" to work "redemption." Boaz, in the Book of Ruth, functioned as a *go'el* to reclaim property for Naomi (Ruth 4:1-12). Jeremiah, as *go'el*, redeemed the land of his cousin Hanamel during the Babylonian siege of Jerusalem (Jeremiah 32:6-15). The term is also applied metaphorically to God a number of times in the Old Testament (see Job 19: 25; Psalms 19:14; 78:35; Isaiah 41:14; 43:14; 54:5; 60:16). While Jesus is never called "redeemer" in the New Testament, he was rightly remembered for his act of redemption (1 Corinthians 1:30; 7:23; Romans 3:24).

The Holiness Code concludes with a long statement of the rewards (Leviticus 26:3-13) and penalties (Leviticus 26:14-33) that accompanied all of God's commandments. Obedience will bring prosperity and security. Disobedience will bring hardship and disaster. Divine punishment will result in the scattering of the people among the nations, thereby ensuring a Sabbath for the land (Leviticus 26:34-39). Even then, if the people confess their iniquity, God will "remember the covenant with the first generation, the ones I brought out of Egypt's land in the sight of all the nations, in order to be their God; I am the LORD" (Leviticus 26:45).

Live the Story

Where do you begin to respond to the challenge to be holy as God is holy? Have you ever thought of yourself as holy? What does it take to be holy? Total perfection? Total purity? If so, clearly no one but God could ever be holy. But the Holiness Code does not call God's people to perfection. Rather, it calls us to imitate God and be holy like God. So how can someone begin to make such an effort? And how can we involve our communities as well?

Perhaps an inventory of the Ten Commandments can provide a starting point. How do you honor God? Do you go to church out of a sense of obligation or in a spirit of expectation and thanksgiving? Are your offerings actually sacrificial; or do they, at least figuratively, consist only of the spare change you have in your pockets or purse? Only you can answer such questions, but honesty before God is the place to start.

What about those commandments that deal with the way we deal with one another? Do you "revere your mother and father" and "rise before the aged, and defer to the old" (Leviticus 19:3, 32, NRSV)? A literalistic execution of these commandments is not the point. Think about how you deal with your elders. Do you offer comfort and empathy as they struggle with growing older? Do you exercise patience when your mother can't move as quickly as she once did or your father becomes confused over details that once were easily handled? The commandments simply offer the place to begin to consider your attitudes and behaviors in order to alter them in your quest to be holy like God.

Use this approach to try to conform to the other commandments as well. Stealing (Leviticus 19:11, 13)? No? Well, how about taking shortcuts in doing your work, paying less than a job is actually worth, or not fully revealing the history of a vehicle you are selling? How about false testimony (Leviticus 19:12, 15-16)? Certainly not! But how about withholding evidence because you don't want to get involved, being swayed by the prominence and/or wealth of someone in the community, or gossiping about another?

By now you get the point: God wants our obedience to surpass the letter of the law and positively affect the way we deal with one another. We are to try to be holy as God is holy. The good news is that God is quite prepared to work with us in becoming the people God desires.

7.

Preparations to Leave Sinai and Hit the Road

Numbers 1:1–22:1

Claim Your Story

What do you do to prepare for a trip? Do you check out the car to see whether it needs maintenance? Do you clean it out, polish the windows, and fill it with gas? Do you use a GPS navigational system to suggest the best route to take? If it is going to be a bike trip, do you check the tires? Do you gather repair tools and make certain you have water? Do you ever take canoe trips or hiking trips? Each of them requires different preparations. Will you go alone, or will you ask someone to go with you? Will the trip be a few hours, all day, or even overnight? What difference does it make?

If the trip is going to be for several days or more, planning gets even more involved. There is the whole matter of what to take in the way of clothing. How long will you be gone? What will you need? What weather is expected? If the trip includes the whole family and children are involved, what can you take along to keep the kids occupied (and semi-quiet)? And, of course, you will need snacks.

The details to consider are seemingly endless. Do you need to take along any medicines, insurance cards, traveler's checks? Who will take care of your pets? Or will you take them with you? And who will care for the houseplants, the yard, or the garden? Will you need to stop the mail? Who needs to let know that you are going to be away? Do people know how to reach you in an emergency? What will you do if—no, when—you realize that you have forgotten something?

Getting ready for a trip takes thought and planning. So it was for Israel as the people prepared to leave Sinai and set out for an uncertain destination.

Enter the Bible Story

Numbers begins with material that most people would consider very boring. Only toward the second half do some of the stories become interesting. To be sure, it is difficult to get excited by lists of people and plans for protection and travel; but the point is that the trip was very well planned. And as the book unfolds, notice how "humanlike" the reactions are to problems and setbacks. Israel's story has continued to engage people across the centuries, in part, because people can see themselves reflected in the narrative.

About the Scripture

Background on the Book of Numbers

The Book of Numbers has three basic parts: the final instructions in the encampment at Sinai (Numbers 1:1–10:10), the long march through the wilderness to the plains of Moab (Numbers 10:11–22:1), and preparation on the plains of Moab for entering Canaan (Numbers 22:2–36:12). Part One and most of Part Two will be the subject of Chapter 7. Because the book begins with a census and then has detailed assignments given to various individuals and tribes—in other words, a lot of "numbers"—the book was named Numbers by those who created the earliest Greek translation, called the Septuagint. In Hebrew tradition, it is known as *Bemidbar* ("in the wilderness," from Numbers 1:1), perhaps a more fitting name, in view of the overall content. Numbers includes a variety of literary traditions, ranging from priestly genealogical lists to stories drawn from the epic story of Israel's history found in the collection of materials we call the Pentateuch, which was put in its final written form most probably in the late sixth century B.C.

Camp Organization and Assignments

The Book of Numbers opens with Moses being instructed by God: "Take a census of the entire Israelite community by their clans and their households, recording the name of every male, 20 years old and above, who is eligible for military service in Israel" (Numbers 1:1-3). Aaron and a select group chosen from the various tribes assisted Moses to determine the number of eligible warriors from each tribe (Numbers 1:4-16). The Levites were treated differently from the rest because of their responsibilities with the tabernacle (Numbers 1:48-54). Following the census is a detailed description of the placement of the various tribal groups surrounding—and thereby guarding—the tabernacle (Numbers 2:1-34).

The numbers of people recorded in the text are surprisingly high. Scholars think that the census numbers may, in fact, represent records from a much later time that were read back into the wilderness context. However that may be, the data reported may reflect very old priestly documents that survived the destruction of Jerusalem in 586 B.C. to be included here when the Pentateuch was completed, late in the sixth century B.C.

Then follow instructions to the sons of Aaron, who will lead the priesthood (Numbers 3:1-4), and a description of the duties of and a census of the Levites (Numbers 3:5-39). The Levites were to serve in substitution for the offering of the firstborn. Additional money payments are authorized should the number of firstborn to be redeemed exceed the number of Levites available (Numbers 3:40-51). The special responsibilities of three Levitical subgroups, the Kohathites, the Gershonites, and the Merarites (4:1-33), are also described and accompanied by a report of a census of their numbers (Numbers 4:34-49).

This is hardly the most exciting part of the biblical narrative. In fact, for most readers, it is tedious. The impression it gives, however, is one of careful attention to detail, to whom can be counted on and what each group is to do. This is the stuff of military planning; this is the stuff of preparation done by thoughtful parents and grandparents; this is the kind of stuff you do before you leave on a trip.

Special Instructions Given Concerning the Priests

To assure the presence of the holy God, it was important to maintain purity within the camp. The priests had special responsibility for these matters. For people who became unclean (Numbers 5:1-4), for determining the guilt or innocence of a woman accused of adultery (Numbers 5:5-31), for persons who assumed nazirite vows (Numbers 6:1-21; not to be confused with the term *Nazarene/Nazorean*, referring to persons from Nazareth; Matthew 2:23; Mark 14:67), special rituals and practices were assigned to the priests. Elaborate provisions for those who would serve in the tabernacle and for the dedication of the tabernacle are recorded (Numbers 7:1-88). The consecration and service of the Levites is also described (Numbers 8:5-23; see also Exodus 29 and Leviticus 8). This apparently applied to only those who were older than twenty-five years old and younger than fifty (Numbers 8:23-26; but see 4:3, 23, 30).

In the midst of this detailed and rather esoteric material is one jewel, the priestly or Aaronic benediction. Among the many responsibilities of the priests were occasions when they pronounced a blessing on the people (see Leviticus 9:22-23; Deuteronomy 10:8; 21:5; Joshua 8:33; Psalm 118:26). The actual wording of those blessings is seldom recorded; but here in Numbers, the tradition of one such blessing has been preserved. It is beautiful in its simplicity. God's care (Numbers 6:24), God's presence (Numbers 6:25), and God's peace (Numbers 6:26) are pronounced. The image of God's "face" and "countenance" are used to refer to divine presence, and God's grace and the shalom (peace/well-being) that it brings is remembered. In the Jewish Study Bible the verses are rendered as follows: "The LORD bless you and protect you! The LORD deal kindly and graciously with you! The LORD bestow His favor upon you and grant you peace!" (Numbers 6:24-26). This blessing offers a summary of what it means to live in God's presence.

The Second Passover and the Departure from Sinai

After all of the details of how the camp was to be organized and all the responsibilities had been assigned, Moses called the people to observe the second Passover, the first since the fateful night on which they prepared to flee from Egypt (Numbers 9:1-4; see Exodus 12–13). This Passover was to take place just prior to their setting out on another journey. They kept the festival in the first month of the liturgical year, on the fourteenth day (Numbers 9:5).

A new situation arose, however, in that some of the people were ritually "unclean" (Numbers 9:6). This was not a problem with the first Passover, since they had not yet received the purity ordinances. In this new situation, these rules had to be applied and yet they had also to have some flexibility. Everyone was expected to participate (Numbers 9:13-14; but see Exodus 12:48). But "unclean" persons and those who happened to be away from the camp for some reason obviously could not. Allowance had to be made. Thus, a second opportunity to celebrate the Passover was scheduled for the following month (Numbers 9:7-12).

From the day that the tabernacle had been erected, the cloud surrounding God's glory "covered the tabernacle, the tent of the covenant; and from evening until morning it was over the tabernacle, having the appearance of fire" (Numbers 9:15-16, NRSV; Exodus 40:34-38). Wherever the cloud settled down, there the Israelites camped and there remained until the cloud lifted and moved to another location (Numbers 9:17-23). Silver trumpets were fashioned by which to summon the people to gather, to warn them of danger, to signal an approaching time of departure, and to announce certain special festivals (Numbers 10:1-10).

On the twentieth day of the second month—six days after the Passover—the cloud lifted and the people set out from Sinai (Numbers 10:11-13). The departure was accomplished in a very orderly manner (Numbers 10:14-28). Moses was able to persuade "Hobab son of Reuel the Midianite, Moses' father-in-law" to go with them because he knew the area and could direct them to sources of water (Numbers 10:29-32, NRSV; Moses' father-in-law was sometimes called Reuel [Exodus 2:18] but was also known as Jethro [Exodus 3:1; 4:18; 18:1-12]).

Two very old pieces of tradition are included in connection with the departure from Sinai of the people and the tabernacle. Both traditions are associated with moving the box-like object called the Ark of the Covenant (Deuteronomy 10:8), the movable shrine into which Moses had placed copies of the Ten Commandments (Exodus 25:16). It was sometimes called the Ark of God or the Ark of the Lord. (This is not to be confused with Noah's ark.) As a piece of "furniture" in the tabernacle, the Ark functioned somewhat like a stand on which was situated the "mercy seat," which served as God's throne when the cloud settled upon the tabernacle (Exodus 25:17-22; Leviticus 16:2). Eventually, King David brought the Ark into Jerusalem (2 Samuel 6); and King Solomon installed it in the Holy of Holies in the Temple (1 Kings 8:4-7). But in earlier times, the Ark of God was taken out as a symbol of divine presence when Israel was on the march. These two battle cries, "Arise, LORD, let your enemies scatter, and those who hate you flee" and "Return, LORD of the ten thousand thousands of Israel" (Numbers 10:35-36), remind us that Israel considered God's presence in a very concrete way.

Discontent on the Road

People seem prone to complain—quickly and loudly—if something goes wrong when they are traveling. We all do it on occasion, and so did Israel on more than one occasion. In such instances when the people voiced their dissatisfaction, God's anger would flare and Moses would intercede (Numbers 11:1-3). The first long account of such discontent found in Numbers sounds very much like a similar story in Exodus (11:4-34; see Exodus 15:22–16:36). In Numbers, "the riffraff among them" (Numbers 11:4; see Exodus 12:38; Leviticus 24:10) along with the Israelites grumbled for want of sufficient food. They longed for the "fish" and the "cucumbers, the melons, the leeks, the onions, and the garlic" that they had had while in Egypt (Numbers 11:5). All they had in the wilderness was manna, and they were tired of that (Numbers 11:6). To Moses' entreaties God then sent more than enough quail to feed the gripers (Numbers 11:10-35).

Even Aaron and Miriam, Moses' brother and sister, got into the drama. They became jealous of Moses' relationship with God. They felt that Moses was less qualified than they because Moses had married a Cushite woman (Numbers 12:1-2). As a result of their challenge to Moses' leadership, Miriam was struck for seven days with a leprous-like skin disease, which was relieved only after Moses interceded for her and for Aaron (Numbers 12:10-16). The principal learning for all that emerged from this incident concerned the very special place that Moses had before God. Unlike just any prophet, the Lord spoke with Moses "face to face—clearly, not in riddles; and he beholds the form of the LORD" (Numbers 12:8, NRSV).

Revolts Against Moses and the Lord

Grumbling was not always enough. Sometimes things turned bitter. The first account involves a group of spies that Moses, at God's direction, sent to explore the land of Canaan (Numbers 13:1-16). They went to see whether the people lived in fortified towns, whether the land was rich or poor, whether there were fruit trees, and so forth (Numbers 13:17-24). What they saw was good, but they reported that the inhabitants were fearsome. They did not believe that the Israelites should go up into the land (Numbers 13:31-32). They said that they [the spies] seemed like "grasshoppers" before the Canaanites (Numbers 13:33).

The people reacted in great fear and complained against Moses and Aaron: " 'If only we had died in the land of Egypt or if only we had died in this desert! Why is the LORD bringing us to this land to fall by the sword? Our wives and our children will be taken by force. Wouldn't it be better for us to return to Egypt?' " (Numbers 14:2-3). Only Caleb and Joshua, who had helped spy out the land, urged the people not to rebel but to do as God directed and go up into the land (Numbers 14:6-9). God was greatly angered by the peoples' stubbornness and unwillingness to trust in God. Had it not been for Moses' intercession, God might well have destroyed them all. As it was, while God did forgive them, none of them except Caleb and Joshua was to be allowed to enter and settle in the land of Canaan (Numbers 14:11-25). After Moses upbraided the people for their lack of trust, they decided to go and launch an invasion of Canaan; it was a disaster (Numbers 14:39-45).

A second revolt occurred when Korah, Dathan, and Abiram challenged Moses' leadership (Numbers 16:1-2). The complaint was that Moses and Aaron had exalted themselves, apparently denying that all of the people of the congregation were holy and had special access to God (Numbers 16:3-4). They also again complained that Moses had brought them out to kill them in the wilderness (Numbers 16:12-14). Moses considered this a revolt against the Lord (Numbers 16:11). To make a longer story short, God was greatly distressed by all of these things and sent an earthquake and a plague among the people (Numbers 16:20-40). Still the people rebelled. Had Moses and Aaron not gone into the midst of the people in intercession, the whole assembly would probably have perished (Numbers 16:41-50). The resulting fear among the people was met by elaborate instructions on a variety of rituals of purification to be conducted on their behalf (Numbers 17:1–19:22).

Nearing the End of the Trip

Approximately forty years passed since the Israelites left Egypt. A number of events had taken place, but none is more puzzling than that reported in chapter twenty. The travelers had reached the large oasis at Kadesh. Miriam, Moses and Aaron's sister, died there (Numbers 20:1). The people once again began complaining and quarreling with Moses and Aaron (Numbers 20:2-5). At divine direction, Moses gathered all of the people with their livestock before a rock. After reprimanding the people for their lack of trust, Moses struck the rock with his rod. Water enough for all gushed forth (Numbers 20:7-12). The place would be called Meribah (Hebrew for "quarrel") because there the people quarreled with God (Numbers 20:13).

The puzzling part of this story is that, for reasons not made clear in the text, Moses and Aaron were both barred from entering the land of Canaan (Numbers 20:12). Indeed, Aaron died soon thereafter (Numbers 20:28), and Moses died while still in Moab (Deuteronomy 34:5). The problem seems to have been that Moses and Aaron "rebelled" by not being patient enough to wait for God to act (Numbers 20:12, 24; 27:14). In other texts, they are said to have uttered "rash" words (Psalm 106:32-33) or to have broken faith with God (Deuteronomy 32:51). Whatever the precise "sin," this incident left a deep mark in Israel's collective memory. Even Moses and Aaron were held responsible before the Lord.

When the company left Kadesh, they were not allowed to pass through Edom (Numbers 20:14-21). As they went around Edom, they encountered opposition at several points. They fought and defeated the Canaanite king of Arad (Numbers 21:1-3). The people once again "spoke against God and Moses" and were punished by a swarm of poisonous serpents (Numbers 21:4-6). When the people repented, God had Moses make the likeness of a poisonous snake in bronze and raise it up so that all who had been bitten could see it and be healed (Numbers 21:7-9). They also were challenged by King Sihon of the Amorites and King Og of Bashan, and they defeated them both (Numbers 21:21-35). Finally, they made their way to "the plains of Moab across the Jordan from Jericho." There they set up camp; that part of the journey was over (Numbers 22:1; 33:48-49; 36:13; Deuteronomy 1:1-5; Joshua 3:1).

Across the Testaments

The Bronze Serpent and Jesus on the Cross

In Numbers 21:7-9, the bronze serpent was a symbol of divine grace and healing. In the Gospel of John, that meaning in the Numbers passage is expanded and employed in reference to the eventual crucifixion of Jesus, which brings healing to the world. " 'And just as Moses lifted up the serpent in the wilderness, so must the Son of Man be lifted up, that whoever believes in him may have eternal life' " (John 3:14-15, NRSV). The image of Jesus being "lifted up" on the cross is found also in John 8:28 and 12:32-34.

Live the Story

The day arrives and the journey actually starts. How are you going to deal with all the unexpected matters that arise? Despite the most careful planning, there will always be the unforeseen. When the kids complain about how long the trip is taking, how will you respond? When you discover that the bottles of water were mistakenly left on the back porch, what will you do? When someone in the family becomes ill, what then? These are some of the contingencies that are simply a part of travel.

In one's life journey, planning is obviously important, but so is flexibility and faith. When the best of plans proves insufficient, will you panic or will you pray? Will you seek the counsel of others traveling along the path, or will you quit in fear or disgust or uncertainty? Israel had to learn to listen and to have confidence that God was with them for their good. As Christ's followers, we have to learn the same things.

What can you do today to strengthen your trust in God? Share your story and get some feedback? Join a group working for social justice in your community? Help reach out to those in your congregation who no longer can get out on their own? Take time each day to study the Bible and pray to God? All or any of these can help you grow in faith and gain in the confidence that God does care for you and wants to be your companion on your life journey.

8.

On the Plains of Moab

Numbers 22:2–36:13

Claim Your Story

Do you ever find yourself torn between competing challenges? Do you want to "think green" but at the same time believe that your family needs a large, less-efficient vehicle? Do you consider loyalty to your school or company to be in competition with your need to take care of yourself or your family? Do you consider civil liberties very important but at the same time believe that any action that might prevent terrorism is justified? Do you think that government is too big but at the same time want government to build better highways and guarantee Social Security benefits?

How do you resolve such conflicting feelings? How do you make up your mind which way to go? Whose opinions do you trust? Do you consider what your denominational church has said on such matters? Do you listen to your local civic leaders? Do your family members have special influence? Do you turn to your Bible for insight?

Life is not usually very neat. There are always conflicts and opposing solutions. How can we keep a sane perspective? How can we find a way to keep from being torn apart by possible choices, of which none is absolutely guaranteed to be right? Is there always one "right" solution to a difficult problem? What do you make of conflicting evidence, particularly from those you especially respect?

The Book of Numbers contains some very troubling accounts, so how are we to benefit from it? Do we ignore it? Do we skip the "bad" parts? Do we pretend that it really doesn't say some of the things it says? What we are talking about is moral judgment and ethics. How do we go about developing our own ethical standards, and how do we adjust them as circumstances change? That is our challenge.

Enter the Bible Story

The plains of Moab, located in what is now modern Jordan, on the east side of the Jordan River, is the geographical setting for the remaining portions of the Book of Numbers. The journey there was long and difficult (see Numbers 33:1-49). After arriving on the plains of Moab, Israel stayed encamped there until the narrative concerning their entry into the land of Canaan commences in the Book of Joshua. A number of interesting, sometimes disturbing accounts are to be found.

Balaam, the Surprising Prophet

Israel's arrival in Moab was not celebrated with joy among the Moabites. Their king, Balak son of Zippor, was quite disturbed because the Israelites "were so numerous" (Numbers 22:3). Thus, he sent messengers to a prophet/diviner/seer, Balaam son of Beor, who lived in what is now Syria, to come and place a curse on the Israelites (Numbers 22:5). King Balak was

Across the Testaments

A Negative View of Balaam

While the Balaam stories in Numbers generally consider the seer favorably (but see Numbers 31:8, 16), elsewhere in the Bible, such is not the case. Balaam's involvement with Balak was generally viewed more negatively than positively (Deuteronomy 23:4-5; Joshua 24:9-10; Nehemiah 13:2; Micah 6:5). Further, the tradition held that Balaam was put to death for divination (Joshua 13:22). In the New Testament, Balaam was described as one who "loved the payment of doing wrong" (2 Peter 2:15). Jude castigated some who were seeking to lead the Christian community as those who "follow the footsteps of Cain....For profit they give themselves over to Balaam's error" (Jude 11). Finally, in the book of Revelation, the people of Pergamum were charged with holding "Balaam's teaching....Balaam had taught Balak to trip up the Israelites, so that they would eat food sacrificed to idols and commit sexual immorality" (Revelation 2:14).

certain that "whomever you [Balaam] bless is blessed, and whomever you curse is cursed" (Numbers 22:6). The elders of Moab and the elders of Midian, the king's envoys, requested that Balaam come with them and place a curse on the Israelites so that Balak would be able to fight against them and drive them out (Numbers 22:7-11). Balaam inquired of the Lord and was told not to go with Balak's messengers or curse the Israelites (Numbers 22:12-14). According to these traditions, Balaam, while not an Israelite prophet, was nonetheless answered in his prayers by the God of Israel.

King Balak was persistent and sent a second group of messengers to Balaam, offering great honor if he would curse Israel (Numbers 22:15-17). Initially, Balaam declined Balak's entreaty; but he did again seek divine guidance (Numbers22:18-19). Lo and behold, God told him to go but to "do only what I tell you to do" (Numbers 22:20). Then in a surprising turn, we are told that God was angry that Balaam was going and so had an angel of the Lord block the way. At first, only Balaam's donkey saw the angel and refused to go ahead. After an exchange between Balaam and his donkey—yes, the donkey's mouth was opened so that he could talk—Balaam finally saw the Lord's angel and realized that the donkey's refusal to move had, in fact, saved Balaam's life. Balaam repented and was prepared to return to his home, but the angel of the Lord repeated God's instruction to go but to do only as God directed (Numbers 22:23-35).

In the ensuing chapters are four oracles attributed to Balaam (Numbers 23:7-10, 19-24; 24:3-9, 15-24). To Balak's consternation, Balaam refused to curse Israel (Numbers 23:8). Rather, he blessed Israel, as instructed by God (Numbers 23:20). Israel was to prosper greatly (Numbers 24:4-7, NRSV) and prevail over all opponents (Numbers 24:8). "Blessed is everyone who blesses you [Israel], and cursed is everyone who curses you" (Numbers 24:9). Moab and Edom, along with the Amalekites and Kenites, were to fall before Israel (Numbers 24:17-24). All of this happened to the surprise and distress of Balak. Balaam's response to the king's despairing inquiries was that he could and would say only what God instructed him to say. He could do nothing else, lest he deny God's Word (Numbers 23:12, 26; 24:2, 13).

This long interlude was no doubt full of humor and of great satisfaction to the original audience. A talking donkey, a thwarted king, assurance of divine protection and blessing. What more could one ask? The stories of Balaam continue to be instructive in that they remind the reader that God is able to speak in quite unexpected ways, even through foreign prophets and their livestock. God's people need always to listen carefully to the content of the messages they receive, without prejudging them on the basis of the identity of the messenger. Sometimes someone outside our "camp" might have something important for us to hear from God.

Preparations for Allotting the Land

One of the major concerns before Israel was how to distribute the land of Canaan that they would soon possess when they crossed over the Jordan River. Thus, another census was taken to determine both the military strength of each tribe as well as the needs of each for land (Numbers 26:2-4). The land was to be apportioned on the basis of the population of each tribe, larger tribes receiving more and smaller tribes less (Numbers 26:52-54). The geographical location assigned to each tribe was to be determined by lot (Numbers 26:55-56). Among those enrolled in the census, none of those adults who originally left Egypt remained, except for Caleb and Joshua (Numbers 26:64-65; see 14:6-9, 30-31).

An interesting problem arose, concerning the daughters of Zelophehad, who belonged to the tribe of Manasseh. According to the census, their father had died, with no sons to inherit his property, but with five daughters: Mahlah, Noah, Hoglah, Milcah, and Tirzah (Numbers 26:33; 27:1). The issue was whether the women should receive an allotment of land. The daughters reasoned that the name of their father should not be removed from his clan by reason of having no sons (Numbers 27:4).

Moses prayed to God and was told that the daughters of Zelophehad should receive the inheritance that belonged to their family. Then a broader ordinance was shaped that dealt with the disposition of the property of any man who had no son, nor daughter, nor brothers (Numbers 27:7-11). A clarification was later made necessary because the possibility arose that if one of daughters of Zelophehad married outside the clan of Manasseh, then the property would pass into the territory of another clan, creating turmoil in the Jubilee year (Numbers 36:3-4; see Leviticus 25:10, 23). The judgment was made that the property would pass to a daughter so long as she married within the clan of her father (Numbers 36:6-8). The ordinance would not apply if the woman married outside the clan because no inheritance could be transferred from one tribe to another, in order that each of the tribes of the Israelites would retain its own inheritance (Numbers 36:6-9). To bring closure to this issue, the narrative reports that all of the daughters of Zelophehad did indeed marry within their clan (Numbers 36:10-12).

In the midst of the issues involving inheritance and the census, we are told that Moses was sent up on a mountain in order to be able to see the expanse of land to be given to Israel (Numbers 27:12). Moses was then reminded that he, like Aaron, was not to be allowed to enter the land because of their behavior "in the wilderness of Zin" (Numbers 27:13-14; see 20:22-29). Therefore, Moses was to take Joshua before the people, in the presence of Eleazar the priest, and commission Joshua to succeed Moses as leader of Israel (Numbers 27:15-20). Interestingly, Eleazar had to confirm Moses' action by casting sacred lots (*urim*) before the Lord (Numbers 27:21). Having done so, Moses then publicly "laid his hands on him [Joshua] and commissioned him" (Numbers 27:23). Joshua became like a second Moses when the people crossed over Jordan and entered Canaan. His story is reported in the Book of Joshua.

Other matters are reported in preparation for entering Canaan. Various types of offerings are described: daily offerings (Numbers 28:1-8); Sabbath offerings (Numbers 28:9-10); monthly offerings (Numbers 28:11-15); Passover offerings (Numbers 28:16-25); offerings for the Festival of Weeks (Numbers 28:26-31); offerings for the Festival of Trumpets (Numbers 29:1-6); offerings for the Day of Atonement (Numbers 29:7-11); and offerings for the Festival of Booths (Numbers 29:12-39). The specifications for the numbers and types or each offering are carefully recorded.

What's more, instructions are given with respect to the fulfilling of any vows made in the course of presenting the various offerings. Any vow a man made was to be carried out (Numbers 30:2). If a woman made a vow, however, the execution of those vows was qualified by her dependency upon a man. For instance, young women still living in the household of their fathers or husbands had to have the agreement of those men to carry out their vows

(Numbers 30:4-9, 11-17). The vow of a widow or a divorced woman, on the other hand, was binding, just as that of a man (Numbers 30:10).

Some of these matters seem strange to contemporary Christians. The inheritance laws and the various sacrifices seem antiquated. The rules concerning the vows made by women seem condescending and demeaning. So how shall they be heard in today's world? At the least, they attest to care for the details of community life. They also suggest that life is intended to be lived with an awareness and regard for God and God's way. In appropriating these teachings for our circumstances, we have to balance them with other portions of the Bible. God's guidance constantly has been tempered by the circumstances God's people faced. As we wrestle with what we are to do to honor God, we need to remember that there are always choices to be made and difficulties that must be considered. One size will seldom fit all.

War With the Midianites

A very disturbing story is told of the origin of a deadly conflict with the Midianites. Apparently, some of the people of Israel began to participate "with Moabite women" in "the sacrifices for their [the Moabites'] god" (Numbers 25:1-2). Some thus "yoked" themselves "with the Baal of Peor," the local manifestation of the Canaanite or the Syrian storm god, known as Baal or Hadad (Numbers 25:3, NRSV). God ordered Moses to execute all of the leaders who had participated (Numbers 25:4-5). At that moment, an Israelite named Zimri son of Salu came with a Midianite woman named Cozbi daughter of Zur (Numbers 25:14-15), whom he had apparently married (Numbers 25:6). How the Moabites and Midianites are connected is not explained, except that the nomadic Midianites perhaps travelled in parts of Moabite territory.

The exact circumstances are not clear. On the one hand, Moses had been told to execute the leaders as punishment for their idolatry; but on the other hand, a plague seems to have fallen on the camp (Numbers 25:9). The plague was relieved when Phinehas, a priest, used a spear to kill both the Israelite man and the Midianite woman (Numbers 25:7-8). From this bloody escapade, Phinehas was blessed with a "covenant of well-being," a "covenant of permanent priesthood" (Numbers 25:12-13). And Moses was instructed to "go after the Midianites and destroy them" (Numbers 25:16-17).

About the Scripture

Who Were the Midianites?

The Midianites, sometimes linked with the Amalekites, were considered among "the people of the East" (Genesis 25:1-2; Judges 6:3, 33). They were a nomadic people who moved through the Syrian and Arabian deserts. At various points in the story of ancient Israel, the Midianites are met. Joseph was sold into slavery by a band of Midianites/Ishmaelites (Genesis 37:25-28, 36). Moses went to Midian when he fled from Pharaoh, was received by Jethro/Reuel, the priest of the Midianites, and married one of Jethro's daughters (Exodus 2:15-21). This same Jethro gave Moses invaluable advice for the administration of judicial matters when Israel was in the wilderness (Exodus 18:17-27). Hobab the Midianite, Moses' brother-in-law, guided Israel in the wilderness (Numbers 10:29-32). Nonetheless, because the Midianites participated in seeking to have Balaam curse Israel (Numbers 22:1-7) and were thought to have led Israel astray at Shittim (Numbers 25:1-15), they became enemies of Israel (Numbers 25:16) and continued so until their defeat by Gideon some many years later (Judges 6:1–8:21). The Amalekites were also considered long-term enemies because of their attack on Israel in the wilderness (Exodus 17:8-16).

At an unspecified later time, memory of this incident was used to encourage the Israelites to attack the Midianites to exact vengeance (Numbers 31:2, 16). A select number of troops were sent to the attack (Numbers 31:3-6). The Israelites were victorious, killing every male, along with the five kings of Midian and Balaam (son of Beor), who apparently counseled the Midianites (Numbers 31:7-8, 16). The Israelites took all of the women and children captive, claimed all of the flocks, and plundered the other valuables as well (Numbers 31:9-11).

When the warriors returned with all their booty, Moses was very upset. He held the Midianite women responsible for the treachery against "the LORD in the affair at Peor." Thus, he ordered the execution of all of the older women and all of the male children, allowing only the young, virgin girls to live and be claimed by the troops (Numbers 31:16-18). Then follow lengthy directions on how the booty was to be divided and a report on the completion of the disposition (Numbers 31:21-53).

There is no way from a contemporary Christian point of view to consider this account as uplifting or exemplary. It is sobering and troubling. It seems to claim divine sanction for a military massacre, and it gives a view of females as little more than property. We cannot simply say OK to such a passage. Rather, we are challenged to decide how we can do better, how we can approach conflict and find peaceable solutions to disagreement. When can war be "justified" and when can it not?

The Cities of Refuge

Several matters fill out the Book of Numbers. The arrangements for the Reubenites, the Gaddites, and the half-tribe of Manasseh (Numbers 34:14-15) to receive land on the eastern side of the Jordan River are described (Numbers 32:1-42). The boundaries of the territory that will be occupied, west of the Jordan River, are noted (Numbers 34:1-12). Tribal leaders are identified (Numbers 34:16-29). And then, there are the cities of refuge.

The people were instructed to build forty-eight cities within their territories in which the Levites (who had no land allotted to them; Numbers 18:20-24) could dwell and work (Numbers 35:1-8). From among those cities, six were to serve as "refuge cities" (Numbers 35:6). Three were to be located east of the Jordan River, in Transjordan, and three west of the river, in Canaan (Numbers 35:14). The purpose of these cities was to provide refuge for persons who might have unintentionally killed someone (Numbers 35:12, 15).

The cities of refuge were designed to neutralize a long-standing practice, that of exacting vengeance for the death of a family member. An avenger was sent to kill the offending person, for the honor of the clan. Intentional murderers were to be executed by this "avenger of blood" (Numbers 35:16-21). The cities of refuge were designed to allow a person safe-haven until guilt or innocence could be demonstrated. The avenger had to allow for a "cooling off" time for all involved. The guilt of a person was to be determined on the basis of at least two or more witnesses (Numbers 35:30). No ransom could be made for the life of a murderer (Numbers 35:31).

Thus, those who accidentally caused the death of another were to have a place of safety until the circumstances of their case could be determined

(Numbers 35:12). Specific situations are cited to illustrate how an unintended death might occur (Numbers 35:22-24). If a person fled to a city of refuge and was then judged "innocent" of intentional murder, that person still had to live in the city of refuge until the death of the high priest who was in office when the death occurred (Numbers 35:25, 28, 32). If the slayer ventured out of the city of refuge before that time and was found by the avenger of blood, then the avenger could kill the slayer and have immunity (Numbers 35:26-27). Murder was not to be tolerated, but neither was blind vengeance.

These were among the many provisions made for life in Canaan, life in a new situation, given to Israel on the plains of Moab (Numbers 36:13).

Live the Story

As you reflect on this chapter, what are some of the issues that you have identified? Probably some are relatively small. How will you resolve the dispute between your children over who gets to use the computer first? Will you gather information about actual needs to use it or will you just arbitrarily decide? Will you set up a schedule so that everyone will know ahead of time who is to do what and when? Such decisions as these are very small versions of the decisions concerning property distribution in Numbers.

Maybe there are some larger issues, such as how you will deal with a move to close the public library or to prohibit children from selling lemonade without a license. Is it necessary for financial reasons to close the library? Is there some kind of health issue with selling lemonade on the street? Who are the major people involved in either decision? Will you go talk with the people at the library and at city hall? What will you do if you find good reasons for upholding each side of the discussion?

The Bible can help, but usually it is in an indirect manner by posing situations about which we can debate appropriate solutions. Do you think that the treatment of women in Numbers is fair? Do you think that it is fitting to slaughter whole populations? Do you think that every passage in the Bible is equally significant? To discuss these matters with others is not a sign of weakness or faithlessness; it is indication of your desire to be a serious follower of Jesus Christ.

Leader Guide

People often view the Bible as a maze of obscure people, places, and events from centuries ago and struggle to relate it to their daily lives. IMMERSION invites us to experience the Bible as a record of God's loving revelation to humankind. These studies recognize our emotional, spiritual, and intellectual needs and welcome us into the Bible story and into deeper faith.

As leader of an IMMERSION group, you will help participants to encounter the Word of God and the God of the Word that will lead to new creation in Christ. You do not have to be an expert to lead; in fact, you will participate with your group in listening to and applying God's life-transforming Word to your lives. You and your group will explore the building blocks of the Christian faith through key stories, people, ideas, and teachings in every book of the Bible. You will also explore the bridges and points of connection between the Old and New Testaments.

Choosing and Using the Bible

The central goal of IMMERSION is engaging the members of your group with the Bible in a way that informs their minds, forms their hearts, and transforms the way they live out their Christian faith. Participants will need this study book and a Bible. IMMERSION is an excellent accompaniment to the Common English Bible (CEB). It shares with the CEB four common aims: clarity of language, faith in the Bible's power to transform lives, the emotional expectation that people will find the love of God, and the rational expectation that people will find the knowledge of God.

Other recommended study Bibles include *The New Interpreter's Study Bible* (NRSV), *The New Oxford Annotated Study Bible* (NRSV), *The HarperCollins Study Bible* (NRSV), the *NIV and TNIV Study Bibles*, and the *Archaeological Study Bible* (NIV). Encourage participants to use more than one translation. *The Message: The Bible in Contemporary Language* is a modern paraphrase of the Bible, based on the original languages. Eugene H. Peterson has created a masterful presentation of the Scripture text, which is best used alongside rather than in place of the CEB or another primary English translation.

One of the most reliable interpreters of the Bible's meaning is the Bible itself. Invite participants first of all to allow Scripture to have its say. Pay attention to context. Ask questions of the text. Read every passage with curiosity, always seeking to answer the basic Who? What? Where? When? and Why? questions.

Bible study groups should also have handy essential reference resources in case someone wants more information or needs clarification on specific words, terms, concepts, places, or people mentioned in the Bible. A Bible dictionary, Bible atlas, concordance, and one-volume Bible commentary together make for a good, basic reference library.

The Leader's Role

An effective leader prepares ahead. This leader guide provides easy to follow, step-by-step suggestions for leading a group. The key task of the leader is to guide discussion and activities that will engage heart and head and will invite faith development. Discussion questions are included, and you may want to add questions posed by you or your group. Here are suggestions for helping your group engage Scripture:

State questions clearly and simply.

Ask questions that move Bible truths from "outside" (dealing with concepts, ideas, or information about a passage) to "inside" (relating to the experiences, hopes, and dreams of the participants).

Work for variety in your questions, including compare and contrast, information recall, motivation, connections, speculation, and evaluation.

Avoid questions that call for yes-or-no responses or answers that are obvious.

Don't be afraid of silence during a discussion. It often yields especially thoughtful comments.

Test questions before using them by attempting to answer them yourself.

When leading a discussion, pay attention to the mood of your group by "listening" with your eyes as well as your ears.

Guidelines for the Group

IMMERSION is designed to promote full engagement with the Bible for the purpose of growing faith and building up Christian community. While much can be gained from individual reading, a group Bible study offers an ideal setting in which to achieve these aims. Encourage participants to bring their Bibles and read from Scripture during the session. Invite participants to consider the following guidelines as they participate in the group:

Respect differences of interpretation and understanding.

Support one another with Christian kindness, compassion, and courtesy.

Listen to others with the goal of understanding rather than agreeing or disagreeing.

Celebrate the opportunity to grow in faith through Bible study.

Approach the Bible as a dialogue partner, open to the possibility of being challenged or changed by God's Word.

Recognize that each person brings unique and valuable life experiences to the group and is an important part of the community.

Reflect theologically—that is, be attentive to three basic questions: What does this say about God? What does this say about me/us? What does this say about the relationship between God and me/us?

Commit to a lived faith response in light of insights you gain from the Bible. In other words, what changes in attitudes (how you believe) or actions (how you behave) are called for by God's Word?

Group Sessions

The group sessions, like the chapters themselves, are built around three sections: "Claim Your Story," "Enter the Bible Story," and "Live the Story." Sessions are designed to move participants from an awareness of their own life story, issues, needs, and experiences into an encounter and dialogue with the story of Scripture and to make decisions integrating their personal stories and the Bible's story.

The session plans in the following pages will provide questions and activities to help your group focus on the particular content of each chapter. In addition to questions and activities, the plans will include chapter title, Scripture, and faith focus.

Here are things to keep in mind for all the sessions:

Prepare Ahead
Study the Scripture, comparing different translations and perhaps a paraphrase.
Read the chapter, and consider what it says about your life and the Scripture.
Gather materials such as large sheets of paper or a markerboard with markers.
Prepare the learning area. Write the faith focus for all to see.

Welcome Participants
Invite participants to greet one another.
Tell them to find one or two people and talk about the faith focus.
Ask: What words stand out for you? Why?

Guide the Session
Look together at "Claim Your Story." Ask participants to give their reactions to the stories and examples given in each chapter. Use questions from the session plan to elicit comments based on personal experiences and insights.

Ask participants to open their Bibles and "Enter the Bible Story." For each portion of Scripture, use questions from the session plan to help participants gain insight into the text and relate it to issues in their own lives.

Step through the activity or questions posed in "Live the Story." Encourage participants to embrace what they have learned and to apply it in their daily lives.

Invite participants to offer their responses or insights about the boxed material in "Across the Testaments," "About the Scripture," and "About the Christian Faith."

Close the Session
Encourage participants to read the following week's Scripture and chapter before the next session.
Offer a closing prayer.

1. Moses and the Confrontation With Pharaoh
Exodus 1:1–11:10

Faith Focus
We see in the liberation of the Hebrews from oppression in Egypt that God works powerfully through different expressions of servant leadership.

Before the Session
If you have not already done so, read all the suggested passages from the Book of Exodus. Scan the story of Joseph in Genesis 37 and 39:1–47:12 so that you can review it for the group. Use a broad-tip marker to print at the top of a large sheet of paper the following heading: "Jacob Brings His Family to Egypt to Escape a Famine in Canaan." Then print the following at the top of a second sheet: "Wanted: Leader to Liberate a People." Post both sheets of paper, along with a blank third sheet, where the group will be able to see them.

Have available a broad-tip marker, paper, pencils or pens, and a markerboard and marker or a chalkboard and chalk.

Claim Your Story
Invite participants to tell about times when they have experienced conflict or controversy in their family, community, workplace, or congregation. How did they react? By ignoring the situation? By waiting for someone else to take charge? By taking the lead themselves in resolving the situation? Has anyone in the group ever found himself or herself drafted, however unwillingly, into a leadership role? Has anyone in the group ever experienced conflict as a time for great growth?

Enter the Bible Story
Ask a volunteer or two to quickly summarize the events in Joseph's life, beginning in Genesis 37 and going through when Joseph's family settles in Egypt. Or do a quick summary yourself. Then ask participants to call out events in order, from the time of Jacob's settling in Egypt through Exodus 1:14, and to list those events under the heading on the first sheet you posted.

Invite participants to pair up. Ask one person in each pair to look at Exodus 1:15-22 and the related material in this study and the other person to look at Exodus 2:1-10 and its related material. Then have each pair discuss the crises in these verses. Who emerged to take the lead? What was surprising about these leaders?

Ask the whole group: Have you ever experienced a time when a leader stepped forward who was surprising or unlikely? In what ways was that leader effective or ineffective in resolving a situation? Do you think that your understanding of what constitutes a good leader differs from God's? In what ways?

Distribute paper and pencils or pens. Call the group's attention to the sheet headed "Wanted: Leader to Liberate a People." Ask participants to jot down what they think would be a job description for a person to lead the Israelites out of slavery. Participants should word their description in a manner such as might appear in the want ads online or in a newspaper. After allowing a few minutes for participants to work individually, work as a group to compose a job description and record it on the posted sheet. Now invite participants to take a few minutes to compose Moses' resume, including his qualifications, experience, and personal qualities. Then on another large sheet of paper, work with the group to compose Moses' resume. Then ask the group to compare the ad with the resume. Is there a match? How can we account for the fact that it was Moses, rather than someone else, who encountered God in the burning bush? What was Moses' response to God's call?

Ask: Have you ever sensed God's call to take a leadership role, perhaps in your congregation? What were your feelings about accepting? Reluctance? A sense of unworthiness or of not being up to the job? How did you respond? Does it make a difference if you have a clear sense of God's presence when you step up to take a leadership role?

Ask volunteers to name the first nine signs and wonders. Then discuss the tenth, the killing of Egyptian first born children. What does it mean that God is involved in the hardening of Pharaoh's heart? Invite the group to name some contemporary despots who have acted with hard hearts. How do their actions reflect the tension between the inscrutable will of God and human freedom of will? Does it make any difference to see the tenth sign's killing of innocents as a response to Pharaoh's edict to kill newborn Hebrew boys?

Live the Story

On a markerboard or chalkboard, print the sentence, "Service is directly related to leadership." In what ways in these first chapters did each of the characters (Shiprah, Puah, Moses' mother and sister, Pharaoh's daughter, Moses) exemplify servant leadership? View the resume for a leader the group composed. Is service reflected there? Do we consider an ability to lead by service when we choose our political leaders or leaders in the workplace? What difference would it make if servant leadership were placed at the forefront of choosing leaders or of accepting leadership roles ourselves? Close with a prayer that we will be open to discerning how we can participate in God's work in the world by being servant leaders.

2. Divine Deliverance and Guidance
Exodus 12:1–18:27

Faith Focus

When we encounter radical changes in our lives and are in great distress, it is natural to feel afraid about what may be ahead. The Israelites' escape from Egypt and their wandering in the wilderness tell us that we are not alone in our fears and that God will sustain us, sometimes in ways we cannot imagine.

Before the Session

Have any participants in your group experienced a catastrophic event such as a fire, tornado, or flood in which they lost most of their possessions or even their home? Allow each person the freedom to choose what he or she is willing to tell about. Provide the space for entering the Exodus narrative without invading the personal space of an individual's difficult experience.

Have on hand paper and pencils or pens.

Claim Your Story

Distribute paper and pencils or pens. Invite the participants to imagine a situation in which they must evacuate their homes in twenty-four hours due to a natural disaster or a war. Each family member may carry one small bag which holds items that the participant chooses. Ask participants to list what they would carry with them. Have the group members discuss their lists.

Then ask the group members to suppose that they have only an hour to evacuate in the face of an encroaching forest fire or an invading army. What would they take? How would one maintain communications with loved ones or make arrangements for elderly persons? If anyone in the group has experienced such a situation, ask him or her to describe what happened if he or she is comfortable doing so.

Then ask the group to suppose that they have escaped from a terrible situation into freedom. Is all now well? What sorts of uncertainties, fears, and unexpected twists of fate might you encounter? Would it ever be possible to wish for the familiar, however difficult it might have been, in the face of the unknown?

Enter the Bible Story

Ask volunteers to tell about family practices or rituals that are uniquely meaningful and why they are meaningful. What stories that accompany these rituals do they tell their children? Ask participants to respond to the following: "When my children ask about _____, I will tell them _____." Jews today include a similar question in the Passover rite, and children are taught to respond by rehearsing the story of the exodus. What do we tell our children about the Lord's Supper?

Divide the group into two smaller groups. Assign to one group Exodus 14:1-31 and to the other Exodus 15:1-18. After several minutes, ask volunteers from each group to summarize the events of the crossing of the Reed Sea, as described in their assigned passage. What are the differences? What seems to be the point of each account?

Call both groups' attention to Exodus 16:1-35, and have someone read the passage aloud. Then invite one group to examine Exodus 15:22-27 and the other group to examine 17:1-7. Invite each group to consider the following questions: What is the attitude of the people when they face new challenges in the wilderness? Whom do they blame? What are they remembering? What do they seem to have forgotten? When we have faced disasters or personal challenges, what has been our response?

The study writer distinguishes between merely hearing and listening. In Hebrew, the same word means "hearing" and "obeying."

Ask: Where in these accounts do the people demonstrate that they hear but do not obey? Have there been times when you faced difficult experiences and sensed God's presence and call, yet you did not obey? What got in the way? Can fear serve as a block between hearing and obeying?

Call the participants' attention to the passage about Jethro's advice and Moses' response.

Ask: Have you ever faced challenges and responded by delegating authority and work to others? Has fear or arrogance ever made you reluctant to let go? What happens in a difficult situation when we try to be God? What happens when we refuse to accept responsibility then expect God to solve our problems?

Live the Story

The writer notes that to be reborn—that is, to rebuild one's life in the face of a radical shift—can be painful as well as wonderful. Being reborn can also be fraught with fear. Invite the group to name practical and theological questions that may arise. How can we demonstrate the presence of God for those who have faced such a trauma? How can we each listen for God's Word and allow ourselves to be receptive to God when we have faced such a life-altering experience?

Close by praying the Lord's Prayer, pausing after the phrase "give us this day our daily bread" to pray silently that we can trust in God's promise to provide and to be there in the face of all of life's uncertainties.

3. God's Covenant With Israel
Exodus 19:1–31:18

Faith Focus

Our covenantal relationship with God comes as a gift of grace. Along with the some-times disturbing recognition that God is truly awesome, we find comfort in the assurance that God cares for us and challenge in what God expects of us.

Before the Session

On a large sheet of paper, print the following three incomplete statements: "I can describe the following about my personal redemption:" "When I evaluate my own life with respect to the Ten Commandments, the following areas come up short:" "When I consider my relationship with God, I am willing to bring the following questions to bear:"

Have available paper, pencils or pens, another large sheet of paper, a broad-tip marker, and a markerboard and marker or a chalkboard and chalk.

Claim Your Story

Invite the participants to name some of the contracts and agreements that are a part of everyday life. List these on a large sheet of paper. For each example named, what are the obligations to which a person agrees? Which of these contracts are relational? In a contract such as marriage, what are the explicit obligations we undertake? What are some implicit promises? What is included in the "fine print" in our relational contracts? Is it possible to always be a promise keeper when we enter into such contractual relationships? What happens when we become contract breakers with our spouse, our child, our business partner, or our friend?

Enter the Bible Story

Invite participants to name God's intentions for the people (Exodus 19:1-7). In response to God's promises, how do the people respond? In preparation for their encounter with God, Moses instructs them to wash their clothes. Ask the group to name a situation where they have entered into a contract. In preparation for this obligation, did they need to leave behind any actions or habits?

Ask participants to close their eyes and imagine that they are a part of the story as someone reads aloud Exodus 19:16-25, the encounter with God identified as a theophany. Discuss: Where were you in this story? What did you see? What did you hear? What were your emotions? In what ways have you experienced God's presence in your life? Were they comforting experiences? Were they frightening? The writer says that we cannot domesticate God. If we view God as only father or friend, do our images limit the divine?

Invite a volunteer to describe the two types of covenant. What kind of covenant is the one described in Exodus? What did God promise, and what did the people agree to do?

Divide the group into two smaller groups. Assign to one group the first four of the Ten Commandments (20:1-11) and to the other the final six commandments (20:12-17). Ask the groups to read the Scripture passage and what the study writer has to say. Ask them to be prepared to respond by naming any new or surprising information and any questions that emerge. Then have the whole group gather to discuss what the small groups discovered.

Invite the group to explore the Covenant Code in Exodus 20:22–23:19; 24:7. Ask volunteers to read aloud the verses that the study writer cites as examples of the ordinances and statutes in the Code. Some of these ordinances and statutes address a settled, agricultural people rather than a people wandering in the wilderness. Invite participants to scan the verses and name some examples. What accounts for this perspective? What would similar ordinances and laws look like that fit the context in which we now live?

Invite the group to scan through the chapters with detailed instructions for constructing a tabernacle and a guide for ordaining priests and for conducting sacrifices. Ask volunteers to read aloud the description of some aspect that particularly strikes them. What accounts for these extremely detailed instructions? What is the importance of this moveable space and the ritual that accompanies it?

Ask a volunteer to read aloud Exodus 31:12-17, about the sanctifying of the Sabbath. Discuss as a group how we observe the Sabbath. Do our actions reflect an understanding that both our space and all of our time belong to God? Which is more important: the spaces in which we worship on the Sabbath or the practices in which we engage on that day of rest? Which of our Sabbath practices honor God? What habits or practices do we engage in that dishonor God?

Live the Story

Distribute paper and pencils or pens to the participants. Call the participants' attention to the incomplete statements you posted before the session. Ask the group to reflect on how they would complete the statements and how they would answer the questions posed in the study. Ask the participants to respond in writing. Encourage the participants to take their responses home to continue to reflect on them.

Close with a prayer giving thanks for God's presence and asking for discernment about ways to increase God's presence in our lives.

4. Disobedience and Forgiveness
Exodus 32:1–40:38

Faith Focus
Like the Israelites in the wilderness, we need to acknowledge the seriousness of our transgressions, humbly ask for forgiveness in word and deed, and trust in God's continuing presence.

Before the Session
Contact two participants and ask them to be prepared to read aloud as a dialogue the roles of God and Moses in Exodus 32:7-13. Also ask your pastor for a prayer of confession. The prayer could be from a denominational worship resource or perhaps the prayer of confession to be used in worship in your congregation in this week's service of worship. Make copies or print it on a large sheet of paper. Also have on hand an additional large sheet of paper and black and red broad-tip markers.

Claim Your Story
Discuss as a group the question of how to tell the difference between making a mistake and being disobedient, using the examples and questions posed by the study writer as a starting point. What are examples of when a person is knowingly disobedient for a particular reason, such as an act of civil disobedience? Should a person who engages in such an act be held accountable nonetheless? Discuss the possible responses a person can make after making a mistake or being disobedient. Does apologizing, making amends, or changing one's behavior wipe out the mistake or act of disobedience? Why, or why not? Must there be consequences? How does an act of disobedience affect a relationship with one who has been wronged by that act? How does it affect our relationship with God?

Enter the Bible Story
Briefly summarize for the group the situation described in Exodus 32:1-7, the making of the golden calf. Then invite the group to listen as the two participants you recruited read Exodus 32:7-13, the dialogue between God and Moses.

After the dialogue, use a red broad-tip marker to print "God" in the center of a large sheet of paper. Then invite participants to call out adjectives that come to mind that describe God's character. Use a black marker to write the adjectives around *God*.

Then ask a volunteer to read aloud verse 14. What does the group make of this indication that God's mind was changed? Is this concept part of their understanding of God's character?

Discuss the disobedient act of making and worshiping a golden calf. Ask a volunteer to read aloud Exodus 32:1. What caused the people to turn away from God? When does uncertainty or fear cause us to turn to something other than God to sustain us? What are the "golden calves" we create? Invite a volunteer to read Exodus 32:21-24. What is Aaron's rationalization for creating the calf? When we have turned away from God and toward material possessions, money, addictions, or status to sustain ourselves, what excuses do we use? Do we ever use "the devil made me do it" as an excuse?

God instructs Moses to prepare a new set of stones to replace the ones he had broken and to ascend to the mountain to receive a new set of tablets. Ask a volunteer to read aloud Exodus 34:6-7, as included in the study under "The Question of God's Accompaniment" (pages 42–43). Then ask volunteers to read, in turn, the passages the study writer includes under "God's Graciousness Described" (page 43).

On the sheet of paper where you wrote adjectives describing God's character, use a red marker to record the seven terms cataloguing God's character. Were any of these among the adjectives that the participants generated? Ask two volunteers to read aloud Exodus 34:8-9 and 34:10-11. What is God's response when Moses asks once again for forgiveness?

We are told that the issue of divine presence was one of deep concern throughout Exodus and that Moses' shining face was a demonstration of both Moses' special relationship with God and of God's continuing presence. Invite the group to reflect on how their lives demonstrate God's presence and the depth of their personal relationship with God. What qualities of our lives shine for others? What aspects of our relationships with other persons testify to God's presence in our lives?

The remainder of Exodus is taken up with the construction and furnishing of the tabernacle and the note that the cloud of God marked God's continuing presence. When the cloud was taken up, it was the indication that the people were to move forward. How does the life of your congregation demonstrate God's presence? When have you experienced in worship the glory of God? When have you discerned that God was nudging you to move forward and out into the world?

Live the Story

Invite the group to consider in silence the ways in which their disobedience has damaged relationships with others and with God. Pray together a prayer of confession.

Close by asking a volunteer to read Exodus 34:6-7 as an assurance of God's continuing presence.

5. Approaching God in Purity
Leviticus 1:1–16:34

Faith Focus

The observance in ancient Israel of animal sacrifice and purity regulations seems strange to us. But the underlying concern for (1) living in ways that do not separate us from God, and (2) the need to be reconciled with God when we do sin, remains relevant for us today.

Before the Session

On a large sheet of paper, print two headings: "Priestly Code" and "Holiness Code." Post the large sheet of paper where the group members will be able to see it. Do some additional research on the Day of Atonement at *www.jewfaq.org.* You will also need chalk and a chalkboard or a marker and a markerboard or another large sheet of paper. Choose a praise song such as "Sanctuary" or "We Bring the Sacrifice of Praise" (found in *The Faith We Sing* and other songbooks as well as on the Internet) that expresses the idea of sacrifice as praise.

Claim Your Story

Invite participants to names things that they hold sacred because of memories or relationships the objects represent. In what special ways do they handle these objects? Are the sacred objects brought out only on special occasions? What objects or occasions did their parents consider sacred? Or what things were they were not allowed to touch or handle when they were children? What sorts of items do participants hold sacred or keep private? What happens when others do not attach the same meaning to an object, an anniversary or a special occasion that participants consider sacred?

Ask for a show of hands of those who have read the entire Book of Leviticus. Does the book seem strange? Is it difficult to understand? This book is about sacred things, so many of the questions the group has just considered may be helpful.

Enter the Bible Story

Review the origin of the book's name. Invite volunteers to read aloud the verses the study writer cites where Aaron and his sons are directly addressed. Besides Aaron and his sons, who is the intended audience? What is the book's purpose?

Call participants' attention to the large sheet of paper with the headings "Priestly Code" and "Holiness Code" that you prepared and posted before the session. Ask the group members to read the sidebar "Two Perspectives on Holiness" (page 50), to name characteristics of each major source of tradition, and to list these under the appropriate heading. Plan to keep this large sheet of paper posted for the next session.

Divide the group into pairs, and assign one of the offerings of thanksgiving to each person. Ask the pairs to review the information in the study and in the relevant verses of Leviticus about their offering. Then have each pair briefly tell the whole group what they discovered.

After the destruction of the Temple, prayers replaced the act of sacrifice as a way of communicating with God. Today prayers and gifts of money are symbols of sacrifice to God. Ask the participants to respond to that idea. How would it change how they enter into prayer or give monetary gifts if they were to view these acts as offering a sacrifice?

Ask participants to look at the information about guilt offerings, sin offerings, and reparations for deliberately violating God's ways. These rituals enabled atonement and made reparations possible, and thus there was grace in this sacrificial system. How do we deal with unintentional or intentional transgressions? Do we have a means for restitution and public confession in our own liturgical life as Christians? Do we, as did the ancient Israelites, view a transgression against a neighbor as a transgression against God? What are we to make of the understanding that the holiness of God is to be taken with utmost seriousness?

Four sources of impurity were to be avoided by following certain ritual rules. The intent was to maintain the purity not only of the tabernacle but of the community as a whole. In our context, what does it mean to maintain purity? What do we see as threats to the purity of our church and our society? Consumerism? Greed? Inattention to the needs of our neighbors? Something else?

Ask a volunteer to summarize the information about the Day of Atonement. Add any additional information you gathered from your research. Print on a chalkboard, marker-board, or large sheet of paper "Atonement." Invite the group to compare and contrast how atonement takes place in Judaism with how we Christians understand atonement. How is God's gracious care for God's people revealed in the Day of Atonement? in the life and death of Jesus Christ?

Live the Story

Invite the participants to think back to the opening exercise and to consider again those things that they identified as sacred. Now ask them to consider places that they view as sacred, and discuss some of the questions posed by the study writer.

Invite the participants to reflect silently on spiritual practices, such as prayer, Bible study, and acts of service and compassion, that can enable them to grow ever closer to God. Because some of the praise music being used in our churches embodies the ideas of prayer and the giving of gifts as sacrifice, close by singing together a praise song such as "Sanctuary" or "We Bring the Sacrifice of Praise."

6. Sanctification and the Holiness of God
Leviticus 17:1–27:34

Faith Focus
Underlying all of ancient Israel's institutions and practices was the command and the desire to be holy as God is holy. We are to imitate God's concern for all that makes and keeps communities healthy, manifesting especially compassionate action for our neighbors who are poor or in need.

Before the Session
Post the sheet of paper headed "Priestly Code" and "Holiness Code" that was used in Session 5. From an old hymnal or from the Internet, get the lyrics to some hymns that focus on Jesus' blood, such as "There Is a Fountain Filled With Blood," "Alas! And Did My Savior Bleed," "Are You Washed in the Blood," or "Nothing But the Blood." Make copies or print the lyrics on a large sheet of paper. (Be sure that the hymn is out of copyright before copying or printing lyrics.) Do some additional research about the six Jewish festivals at *www.jewfaq.org*.

On ten separate large sheets of paper, print each of the Ten Commandments. Provide a broad-tip marker for each sheet. Get copies of the Argentinean praise song "Santo, Santo, Santo," found in *The Faith We Sing* and elsewhere, or a hymn such as "Holy, Holy, Holy! Lord God Almighty," "Take Time to Be Holy," or "Lord, I Want to Be a Christian."

Claim Your Story
Invite participants to recall the conversation from the last session about what is sacred to them. What were some of the things they named? Would participants agree that one can distinguish between something being "sacred" and something being "holy" by how the value is understood? The study writer notes that in Leviticus, the slight distinction between the two terms is that sacred rituals are defined by God and relationships are made sacred by the divine presence.

Enter the Bible Story
Call the group's attention to the large sheet of paper with the Priestly Code and the Holiness Code. In this section of Leviticus that comprises the Holiness Code, the community of Israel and its relationship with the Holy One is the primary focus.

Ask volunteers to read aloud Leviticus 17:13; 16:14-15, 18, and 27. The Hebrews considered blood to be the source of power for animals, including humans. Look together at the hymn lyrics focusing on the blood of Jesus. How does the group respond to these images (some of them graphic)? Note that the significance of blood in these verses of Leviticus has to do with prohibitions against practices and customs that could lead the people away from God and toward worshiping other gods. What customs and practices today can lead us away from God?

Explain that Leviticus 18 and 20 provide the envelope that surrounds Leviticus's rendering of the Ten Commandments—the context for how God expects the people to be holy. Note that the prohibitions in chapter 19 against certain sexual acts seem to be connected with the worship of fertility deities and therefore a violation of the first commandment.

Ask a volunteer to read aloud Leviticus 19:17-18. Would group members agree that this is at the heart of all actions that move us toward being holy as God is holy? The special rules for those who become priests contain some troublesome prohibitions. What expectations do we have today for those who serve us as pastors and in other offices of the church? Call the group's attention to the information about the six annual Jewish festivals, and add additional information from your research. In what ways do these festivals provide touchstones for faithful life for Jews? How does our liturgical calendar provide a framework for our lives as Christians?

Ask the participants to pair up, with one person reading the material about the Sabbatical Year and one the Year of Jubilee and then sharing the information with each other. Point out that the year 2000 was declared a year of Jubilee by many groups who urged that the heavy indebtedness of developing countries be forgiven. What would be the implications of enacting Jubilee today? How might we view some critical issues we are facing if we viewed ourselves as "immigrants and foreign guests," as the Hebrew people were viewed by God? What if we took seriously both Jubilee and the imperative to love our neighbor as ourselves? The Holiness Code takes the position that obedience will be rewarded and disobedience punished. How do participants respond?

Live the Story

Invite the group to take inventory of the Ten Commandments, as suggested in the study. Have participants help you post around the room the large sheets of paper with the Ten Commandments. Then invite the participants to move around the room, reading each commandment and reflecting on the questions about it that were posed in the study. Ask the participants to record on the sheet any comments and further questions they have. Ask them to also read the comments and questions others have recorded. When everyone has had a chance to reflect on all ten, close by singing a praise song or hymn about holiness.

7. Preparations to Leave Sinai and Hit the Road
Numbers1:1–22:1

Faith Focus
Like that of Israel on the long journey in the wilderness, our trust in God sometimes falters when the unexpected happens. But God is worthy of our trust in all circumstances.

Before the Session
On a large sheet of paper, list the three parts of the Book of Numbers from the sidebar "Background on the Book of Numbers" (page 70). Have on hand paper, pencils or pens, drawing paper, and various colors of markers or pencils for each participant.

Claim Your Story
Invite participants to think about a trip they have recently taken, whether an extended road trip, one that involved a flight, or a camping or bike trip. Distribute paper and pencils or pens, and ask the participants to jot down the various preparations they made for the trip. In the total group, ask volunteers to talk about their lists. In addition to the physical preparations they made, what kind of emotional preparation was involved? Did anyone have to mentally let go of tasks and worries of their normal day-to-day lives? Did unknown factors cause anxieties, such as those that might be present if going for a job interview or embarking on a journey to arrange a new living arrangement for an elderly relative? Not only thought and planning, but also uncertainties were involved for the people as they prepared to leave Sinai.

Enter the Bible Story
Call the attention of participants to the sheet with the three parts of Numbers. Review the information in the sidebar "Background on the Book of Numbers" that describes the contents of the book and the origin of its name. Invite the group to scan the information under the heads "Camp Organization and Assignments" and "Special Instructions Given Concerning the Priests." What details strike them? What is interesting or noteworthy, or provokes a question?

Invite the group to consider the events in the next four sections as the outline for a movie or play. Assign the following scenes to individuals (or pairs or small groups, depending on the size of your group): Passover and those who were unclean; the cloud and the fire; the Ark of the Covenant; grumbling about food; the jealousy of Miriam and Aaron; spies exploring the land of Canaan; the challenge of Korah, Dathan, and Abiram; water from a rock; Moses and Aaron being banned from entering Canaan; the bronze serpent.

Distribute drawing paper and colored markers or pencils. Invite the participants to make a storyboard about their assigned incident. They might make simple drawings or use symbols or words to provide just a hint of what happened. When everyone has had a chance to finish, ask the participants to display their storyboard and explain it. What do these incidents portray about the journey the people were on? When have you felt that you were wandering in the wilderness? How did you respond? with fear? by grumbling? by telling others about your sense of uncertainty? To whom did you look for guidance? In wilderness times, what sustains your trust and faith in God?

Live the Story

Invite the group to consider again their list of preparations for the trip. What preparations or details had been forgotten? Were there unexpected circumstances that caused changes in your plans? If so, how did you respond?

Ask the participants to now consider their life journey. While planning is important for life's journey, flexibility and faith are also key. Distribute paper and pencils again. Invite participants to draw a horizontal line on the paper that represents their life journey to this point. Ask them to note at intervals along the line important life events, such as graduation, marriage, the birth of a child, a first job, or other events. Also ask them to record events that were difficult or unexpected—places where the path was rough or interrupted or painful, where it felt like a wilderness experience.

Then ask the participants to consider the questions in the next-to-last paragraph of the study in terms of past events. (For example, did you panic or pray in the face of an unexpected obstacle?)

The study writer observes that Israel experienced God's presence in very concrete ways. They were guided by the cloud of presence by day and the pillar of fire by night. Invite the participants to reflect on the questions in the last paragraph, considering what they might do to strengthen their trust in God and increase their sense of God's very real presence guiding them. What spiritual practices—prayer; Scripture reading; acts of compassion, justice, mercy, or extending hospitality—can they begin to do or increase the time and energy they devote to God?

Close by praying that God will guide you in taking steps to grow in trust in God. Then read the Aaronic benediction.

8. On the Plains of Moab
Numbers 22:2–36:13

Faith Focus
Sometimes the Bible is helpful to our decision-making only indirectly, not by providing us with examples to mimic, but by posing situations about which we can debate appropriate responses.

Before the Session
Set up your learning space with chairs in a large circle that leaves space for a smaller circle of six chairs (placed with their backs to the center) in the middle for the fishbowl activity. Have on hand paper and pencils or pens.

Claim Your Story
Invite each participant to read the competing challenges posed by the study writer and to choose one that resonates with him or her. If a participant finds that none of these challenges applies, have him or her to identify one of his or her own. Then ask that the participants read in the second paragraph the questions about resolving conflicting perspectives. What criteria do the participants use—some of those suggested by the study writer or something else?

Ask the participants to give their opinions about what to do with troubling accounts, whether in Numbers or in another biblical account. The writer suggests that we need to find ways to develop our own ethical standards and then learn how to adjust them as circumstances change. How does the group respond to the writer's suggestion?

Enter the Bible Story
Ask the participants to read silently Numbers 22 and the information in the study about Balaam. Then assign volunteers the parts of King Balak, Balaam, Balaam's donkey, the angel, and the elders of Moab and Midian (this could be several persons). Place six chairs in a tight circle in the center of the room and encourage the rest of the group to sit in chairs in a circle around it. Invite Balak, Balaam, and an elder of Midian to take a seat in the inner circle, which functions as a fishbowl. Then ask the characters to begin a discussion about what happened in this account. After a few minutes invite the donkey and the angel to join the circle. Other elders or participants from the outer circle can take an empty chair and join the discussion at any time. When the conversation runs its course, debrief the exercise. What messages from God were coming through in this narrative? Why do you suppose God chose to speak through the donkey? Have you ever experienced hearing something that seemed to be of God from an unexpected source—someone outside the circle? How do you evaluate messages coming from unexpected sources?

Review the preparations made to enter Canaan, asking volunteers to explain briefly the inheritance laws, the rules about vows made in the course of presenting offerings and the various offerings. Which rules or laws seem to be practical today? Which are antiquated? Which are disturbing? Why? These rules and regulations attest to the care taken for the details of the community's life and suggest that life should be lived with an awareness of God and of living in God's way. What aspects of our life as a community of faith reflect rules, spoken or unspoken, that bind us together as Christ's body? Do our practices and customs reflect an awareness of living in God's way? What Scripture passages counter some of the more disturbing elements of these verses and of the story of the massacre of the Midianites?

Review the information about the cities of refuge. How did these cities function, and what was their purpose? In what way did these cities reflect how to deal with murder and the desire to exact vengeance? Is there a need for a city of refuge today? Do we need ways to balance the conflicting interests and perspectives on polarizing issues that tend to immobilize people of good will?

Live the Story

Invite the participants to choose an issue or a situation about which they feel torn by conflicting challenges. They may choose one delineated by the study writer or another one about which they feel conflicted. Distribute paper and pencils or pens and invite the participants to list the pros and cons on the issue or situation they chose. Then ask them to reflect on what criteria they will use for coming down on one side or another. To whom do they go for advice? How do they use Scripture for discernment? What role does the community play in helping them make a decision? What if there is no right answer? Are there overarching biblical themes that can be helpful, for example, the rule of loving neighbor as one loves the self, considered in the last session?

If time permits, ask someone to put forth his or her issue for discussion. Spend a few minutes listening to each person's input.

Then close with prayer, giving thanks for God's presence and asking for guidance in discerning answer for this issue and for all of the other troubling and difficult decisions of our lives.